D1244418

DUCATI 4-VALVE V-TWINS

DUCATI
4-Valve V-Twins
The Complete Story

Mick Walker

The Crowood Press

First published in 1999 by
The Crowood Press Ltd
Ramsbury, Marlborough
Wiltshire SN8 2HR

British Library Cataloguing-in-Publication Data
A catalogue record for this book is available from the British
Library.

ISBN 1 86126 244 2

Dedication
To the memory of my son Gary, who died whilst competing in
the sport he loved.

Typeface used: New Century Schoolbook.

Typeset and designed by
D & N Publishing
Membury Business Park, Lambourn Woodlands
Hungerford, Berkshire.

Printed and bound by The Bath Press.

Contents

Acknowledgements

My first Ducati, a 250 Daytona (the second imported into Britain), was bought in the spring of 1961. Since then my loyalty towards the Bologna marque has stayed with me. The intervening decades have seen Ducati fortunes rise and tumble more than once, but the last decade has seen most change.

Like that other great love of my life, Alfa Romeo, Ducati have benefited in recent times from first the Cagiva take-over and much more recently from the Texas Pacific Group's involvement. Again the parallel with Alfa is clear – the Fiat take-over of Alfa in the late 1980s brought about a much-

The author with the Foggy Replica he tested in August 1998. The smile says it all!

Where the hell did I leave my Ducati? A scene from the 1993 World Super Bike round at Donington Park.

needed modernization process and huge leaps forward in quality control. But both Ducati and Alfa Romeo have managed to retain that individuality – charisma if you will – so beloved of enthusiasts for both these Italian brands.

Even since my first book, *Ducati Singles* (Osprey, 1985), I have always tried to present a true picture of the marque and its products. This respect for truth has often led me to criticize both the product *and* the factory's management. In *Ducati Four-Valve V-Twins* this has proved far more difficult, as both the motorcycles and the management of the company have improved to levels that would have seemed totally impossible even a few short years ago. In describing the legendary 250 Mach 1 single of the mid-1960s, I once described it 'as a masterpiece dressed in tatters' (referring to its thin paint and peel-off chrome). But with the latest machines, such as the 996 Hyper Sports and ST4 sport-tourer, the level of finish approaches the best that Japan can produce, whilst the dynamics are simply out of this world.

My thanks go to so many who have helped make this book possible, but perhaps most of all to Rod Woolnough. Next in line are the current British importers, Moto Cinelli, including not only boss Hoss Elm, but also Peter Brooking, Jeff Green, Iain Rhodes, Paul Graves, Dave and Luke Plummer, and last but not least, Georgina Jonas. Members of the Ducati's Owners Club (GB), including David Harvey and Jilly Peneger, helped with their continuing enthusiasm and support.

Besides the factory and my own collection, illustrations came from a variety of sources, including James Arnold, Garry Clarke, Doug Jackson, Neil Emmott, Phil Masters, Roland Brown, Vic Bates, David Goldman, Oli Tennent, Patrick Gosling, and Gerolamo Bettoni.

Mick Walker
Wisbech, Cambridgeshire
June 1999

1 The History of Ducati

The story of the four-valve Ducati starts in 1985; first of all, however, there follows a year-by-year guide to the company's history from 1922 to the start of the four-valve story.

1922

A nineteen-year-old physics student, Adriano Ducati, begins experiments with radio transmitters.

1925

Adriano, joined by his brothers Marcello and Bruno Cavalieri Ducati together with Carlo Crespi, founds the Societa Scientifa Radio company.

1936

The Ducati radio and electrical works employ nearly 11,000 employees in their various factories.

1940

A new, modern factory at Borgo Panigale on the outskirts of Bologna is opened, employing almost 10,000 workers, manufacturing optical and engineering products.

1945

Virtually all Ducati's various production facilities lie in ruins following heavy Allied bombing in the north of Italy. Turin lawyer Aldo Farinelli designs the Cucciolo (Little Pup) 48cc auxiliary engine, which can be fitted to a conventional pedal cycle.

1946

The Cucciolo engine enters production at Ducati's Borgo Panigale factory in Bologna. Originally this was built under licence from Siata in Turin. Over 250,000 were subsequently to be built by Ducati and exported all over the world.

1948

Ducati engineers redesign the Cucciolo engine under the designation T2.

1950

The first complete Ducati motorcycle, using a 60cc version of the Cucciolo engine with three-speed transmission, makes its debut. This landmark in the Bologna company's history was just the start, with a succession of models coming on stream over the next few years.

1951

A specially prepared Cucciolo runs for 48 hours non-stop, setting twenty-seven new world records for its class, including the 24 hours for machines up to 100cc. This follows the lead set by Ugo Tamarozzi, who had broken twelve records the previous year on a similar machine.

1952

The Cruiser, a 175cc scooter with ohv engine and automatic transmission, enters production. Although it is of an advanced design, its high price and weight restrict sales. Styled by Ghia.

(Above) *Production of the 48cc Cucciolo (Little Pup) auxiliary motor began in 1946; later in 1948 Ducati engineers redesigned it under the designation T2. Over 250,000 of these tiny four-stroke engines were sold world-wide over the next few years.*

Designed by the famous Ghia studio, the 175 Cruiser featured an ohv engine and automatic transmission; however, although it had an advanced design it was too complex and expensive. Only 2,000 were sold.

1953

Ducati splits into two separate groups: Ducati Meccanica (motorcycles and other mechanical vehicles and engines) and Ducati Elettrotecnica (electrical). Giuseppe Montano is appointed head of the Meccanica division.

1954

Ducati enter a three-man squad in the ISDT (International Six Days Trial), held that year in Wales. As the smallest machines in the event, they generate considerable interest.

The Ducati line-up from their 1955 catalogue, including various Cucciolo-engined mopeds, 65, 98 and 125cc pushrod lightweight motorcycles and the brand new that year ohc 98 Gran Sport, the latter being Ing. Fabio Taglioni's first design for the Bologna factory.

1955

On 1 May Ingegnere Fabio Taglioni is appointed chief designer. His first design is the 98cc Gran Sport (which became known as Marianna).

1956

In May, Degli Antoni debuts the dohc 125GP racer at the Faenza circuit. Then, in July of that year, the same rider makes a stunning debut on the new 125 Desmo in the Swedish Grand Prix – lapping the entire field at least once on his way to victory. The 175 Sport, the first of the street models to be developed from Taglioni's bevel ohc single layout, is a major attraction of the Milan Show in November. Mario Carini and Santo Ciceri break over forty world records at Monza the same month on a streamlined 98 Gran Sport.

Piloting a fully streamlined 98 Gran Sport ohc single, Mario Carini and Santo Ciceri smashed no fewer than forty-one world records at Monza in November 1956, on the eve of that year's Milan Show.

1957

The final running of the world-famous Moto Giro (Tour of Italy) and Milano–Taranto long-distance road races takes place – killed off by fatal accidents during the automobile Mille Miglia the same year. Leopoldo Tartarini and Giorgio Monetti begin a 60,000km (37,300 mile) round-the-world marathon on a 175 Turismo in September; a year later, in September 1958, the duo make a triumphant return to Bologna, having visited no fewer than forty-two countries and five continents.

1958

Ducati make a full-blown attack on the 125cc road-racing world championships; Alberto Gandossi finishes runner-up in the series. Ducati win in Belgium, Sweden and at Monza; at the latter venue they blitz the field to take the first five places. On the production front the 200 Elite makes its debut and is to prove even more popular than the 175 model.

1959

Young Englishman Mike Hailwood wins his first ever Grand Prix (the Ulster) aboard one of Taglioni's 125 Desmo singles. Mike goes on to finish third in the world championships that year. Ducati begin selling motorcycles in the USA, via the Berliner Motor Corporation of New Jersey. At the end of the year Ducati strike the first of their many financial problems.

Ing. Fabio Taglioni with a cylinder head from one of his 125 Desmo single-cylinder racing motorcycles, circa 1958.

(Below) *The latest and largest overhead cam bevel single to enter production at Ducati when it was launched in 1958, the 203cc (67 × 57.58mm) Elite. It helped establish Ducati in export markets.*

Mike Hailwood with his new 250 Desmo twin at Silverstone in April 1960. Built just when Ducati were closing their racing development programme, the type never reached its full potential.

1960

Just as the factory race department is being shut (due to financial considerations), British importer Stan Hailwood (Mike's father) persuades Ducati to build 250 and 350cc Desmo racing twins for Mike to ride. This first twin, a 175, had debuted in 1957, and a 125 the following year. In truth, none were to meet expectations.

1961

The first full-size 250 Ducati single enters production in the shape of the Diana

(Below) *Ducati's first full-size 250, the Diana (Daytona in the UK) debuted in the spring of 1961 to huge public acclaim.*

The three-speed Puma moped was one of several Ducati models to sport a 48cc two-stroke engine. This is the 1963 model.

(Daytona in the UK). This was soon to be followed by the Monza (touring) and Scrambler (on-off road) versions. Also to take advantage of the new Italian highway code (which allowed restricted 50cc machines on the road with no number-plate, licence and so on), Ducati introduce their first two-stroke models, powered by a 48cc piston port engine in either single-speed or three-speed form.

1963

Ducati return to the scooter world when they present the Brio 48 (powered by one of the three-speed moped engines) at the Milan Show that year, followed by a 100cc version a year later. But the *nuovo* scooters are to prove no more successful than the Cruiser of a decade earlier. At the other end of the scale Taglioni designs the massive 1,257cc V-four Apollo for the American importers Berliner. It never enters production.

1964

A prototype 285cc Mach1/S wins the Barcelona 24-hour race ridden by Bruno Spaggiari and Giuseppe Mandolini. Later that summer the 248cc Mach 1 goes on sale. Capable of 100mph (160km/h), it sports a 29mm Dell'Orto racing carburettor, five speeds and 30bhp. Sixties youth love it, but cannot afford the price tag.

1965

Engineer, factory test rider and racer Franco Farné tests Ing. Taglioni's 125 four. First designed in the early 1960s, by the time it is finished Honda have raised the stakes with a five-cylinder model, so the Ducati ends its days touring the exhibitions of Europe. Years later it is discovered in, of all places, Riga, the capital of Latvia, before being returned to Italy in the early 1990s.

1968

The first of the 'widecase' singles appears in the shape of the 350 Mark 3, soon followed by a 250 version, plus Scrambler and Desmo versions.

1969

The 'widecase' theme broadens to include not only 250 and 350cc bikes, but a brand-new 450 (actually 436cc). But Ducati are in deep financial trouble and this time the long-serving Dr Montano is removed from office and a large cash injection made by the Italian government to stave off the possibility of bankruptcy.

Ing. Fabio Taglioni (left) with the 125 four-cylinder racer tested by Franco Farné (right) during 1965.

With the introduction of 250 and 350cc widecase singles the year before, in 1969 Ducati brought out a brand new 450 (actually 436cc). It was offered in Mark 3, Scrambler and Desmo versions; a brochure photograph for one of the first is shown here.

1970

With the new government-appointed management of Arnaldo Milvio and Fredmano Spairani in place, chief designer Fabio Taglioni is given the green light to design a brand-new large capacity model. The prototype appears in August in the shape of a 750 90-degree V-twin with bevel-driven single overhead camshafts.

1971

Limited production of the new V-twin begins, now known as the 750GT. The top-selling Ducati model this year is the single-cylinder Scrambler series. A prototype 500 GP V-twin is built on the lines of the production 750.

1972

The year of Ducati's great Imola triumph, when Paul Smart and Bruno Spaggiari create a sensation by finishing first and second respectively against the cream of the racing world, including Agostini and MV Agusta. A new version of the 750, the Sport, makes its debut towards the end of the year.

1973

Often a happy hunting ground for Ducati over the years, Montjuic Park, Barcelona, is the setting for the debut of the 860. The Spanish pairing of Benjamin Grau and Salvador Canellas not only wins, but manages to tuck in more laps than anyone before them. The 750 Sport enters production.

1974

This was the last year of the singles and the 750 round-case bevel V-twins. The beautiful, exotic 750SS goes on sale, a total of 450 being constructed.

1975

A disastrous year, with the 125 Regolarita (two-stroke enduro), 350/500 GTL (parallel twins) and the Giugiaro-styled 860 GT V-twin all proving notable sales flops. Only the 900 SS sporter, using a Desmo version of the GT engine, saves management blushes.

(Above) *The day that first brought the Ducati V-twin to the public's attention – 23 May 1972. Paul Smart (16) and team-mate Bruno Spaggiari score an amazing 1–2 victory against the cream of superbike racing at the Imola circuit.*

In July 1973 Salvador Canellas (left) and Benjamin Grau (on bike) won the gruelling 24 Horas (hours) endurance race at Montjuic Park, Barcelona, at record speed, riding the prototype 860 Ducati V-twin.

(Opposite, top) *The last year Ducati produced their 750 GT V-twin (foreground) and the Desmo single (background) was 1974. Both motorcycles were to be sadly missed by their many admirers around the world.*

(Opposite, below) *The round case 750 V-twin was replaced by the square style (and many would say ugly) 860 GT. The work of car styling house Ital (Giugiaro), it, and other new bikes including a 125 two-stroke enduro and a couple of parallel twins, all proved major sales flops.*

Mike Hailwood made an amazing comeback to racing at the 1978 Isle of Man TT. Riding an NCR Ducati 900 entered by Sports Motorcycles, 'Mike-the-bike' won the Formula 1 event and with it the F1 world title – Ducati's first. He is seen here (right) with John Williams on the podium after his victory.

(Above) *Only the SS (Super Sport) Desmo V-twins saved Ducati's fortunes. This 900 SS, being ridden in the 1976 Isle of Man Production TT by Malcolm Wheeler, was entered by former 350cc world champion Freddie Frith.*

1976

First displayed at the Bologna Show in December 1976, the 900 Darmah is styled by Tartarini, who earlier the same year was responsible for the Sport Desmo 350/500 parallel twin series.

1977

The first belt-driven engines appear in prototype form, in the shape of a single-cylinder 350 and a 500 90-degree V-twin. Both are the work of Fabio Taglioni.

1978

The year Mike Hailwood makes his triumphant comeback. Riding a 900 NCR racer the Englishman not only wins his race over the arduous Isle of Man TT course, but with

The trend-setting 500 SL Pantah entered production in 1979. Its belt-driven overhead camshafts set Ducati on a new course, and one they remain on to this very day albeit with the added advantages of liquid cooling, dohc and electronic fuel injection on the four-valve models.

(Below) *The 600 SL Pantah arrived in 1981; it was the first production Ducati to boast a hydraulic clutch.*

it the TTI World Championship on 2 June. NCR worked closely with Ducati for almost three decades. Owners Rino Caracchi and Giorgio Nepoti finally retired in 1995.

1979

The first standard production Ducati with belt-driven overhead cams goes on sale in the shape of the 500 SL Pantah V-twin. This is the father of all modern Ducati Vs, including the four-valve line. And to celebrate the first world title, the factory produces the Mike Hailwood Replica 900. Originally planned as a one-off exercise, it proves so popular that during the early 1980s it becomes Ducati's best-selling model.

1981

Ducati win their second world title, thanks to the 600 TTF2 Pantah-based racer and its rider, Tony Rutter. This pairing go on to win three more world championships (1982, '83 and '84). A 600 Pantah (the SL) goes into production for the street, the first production Ducati to use a hydraulic clutch.

Englishman Tony Rutter won no fewer than four TT F2 world titles on a racing version of the 600 Pantah V-twin: in 1981, '82, '83 and '84.

1982

The last of the old-style bevel SS V-twins is built, in the shape of the 900 SS. Sales of Ducati motorcycles world-wide fall to an all-time low.

1983

A year of turmoil. Ducati is still owned by the Italian government and part of the VM Group via the state financial institution Societa Finmeccanica. First the 900 S2 replaces the much-loved SS, then in June come the first contacts with Cagiva, initially to supply Ducati V-twin engines for fitment into Cagiva motorcycles. New versions of the Pantah appear – the 600 TL and XL350.

1984

Cagiva begin work on the Elefant 650 with a Pantah engine, whilst at the end of the year a new 1,000cc version of the famous bevel V-twin arrives, the Mille, with many revisions, including plain-bearing big-ends.

Cagiva began to develop an off-road machine to take part in such gruelling events as the Paris–Dakar Rally; this 650 Pantah-engined machine is an early version of what was later to be known as the Elefant.

1985

On 1 May Cagiva take over Ducati, and so after four decades the company reverts to private ownership and a new era is born.

The 750F1 of 1985 was to be the last model developed under the old government-supported Ducati company. Cagiva officially took over Ducati on 1 May 1985.

2 Four-Valves Arrive

During his thirty-year tenure as Ducati chief designer, Ing. Fabio Taglioni achieved many great things. It was he, of course, who created the L-shaped (90-degree) V-twin, at first with bevel-driven, and later belt-driven, overhead camshafts, added to the famed desmodromic (Desmo for short) valve operation. But there were significant areas in which this great man showed virtually no interest at all, especially the four-valves-per-cylinder option, liquid cooling and fuel injection. Instead it was left to Taglioni's successor, Massimo Bordi, to exploit these three important features.

Born in Bevagna, Perugia, on 9 May 1948, Bordi had from an early age shown a flair for mechanical engineering. And it would be true to say that his inspirational figure was Taglioni – the young Massimo was to earn his degree in mathematical engineering with, of all things, a thesis outlining the advantages of the desmodromic valve system for four-stroke engines. After gaining his university degree in 1974, he joined Ducati in January 1978, following previous employment first as a teacher and later as a quality controller at Terni SpA.

As subsequent events were to prove, the now fully qualified *Ingegnere* (engineer) was a perfect choice to follow in the footsteps of Taglioni. Unlike many men who would simply have gone for a total 'new sheet' approach, Massimo Bordi took on board the established design formula, studying instead ways in which this could be updated to take on the challenge of the future, and at the same time making sensible and practical improvements. He realized that if he could further advance the basic L-shaped V-twin, with its desmodromically operated valves and near perfect 90-degree configuration, he would have the makings of an engine that could take on and beat the best in the world – for both street and track use. He foresaw four main areas of improvement: multi-valves, double overhead camshafts, liquid cooling and fuel injection.

Bordi also made contact with several Italian and foreign companies specializing in

'4 valves DOHC' on the fuel tank above the Ducati logo tells the story on the original racing prototype model in Misano in April 1987.

multi-valve technology and fuel injection systems. Perhaps most notable of these concerns was the British Cosworth engineering group, headed by director Keith Duckworth.

During the early 1980s, at the time when Bordi was learning his way around, no other mainstream Italian motorcycle manufacturer was actively seeking out modern technology. Consequently, with the Cagiva takeover in May 1985 and their vast increase in funding – and enthusiasm – Bordi's concept of a new era V-twin engine was given full reign. (In fact one of the Castiglioni brothers' – Claudio – first actions was to authorize work to begin on the project that would ultimately break cover as the 851 Superbike, in a mass of media attention at the Milan Show in November 1987.)

PROTOTYPES

But before the definitive production version made its debut came a series of prototype engines, the first of which simply incorporated a water-cooled top section above a pair of modified Pantah crankcases. The crankcase modification centred around the relocation of the cylinder through-studs, which were moved outwards to allow for the anticipated larger bore sizes and liquid cooling. At first the engine size was restricted to 748cc (88 × 61.5mm) – the same as on the 750 F1 and the Paso (the latter being introduced at Milan at the end of 1985).

Development was not just restricted to bench testing, but extended road tests and even track testing. The latter including the

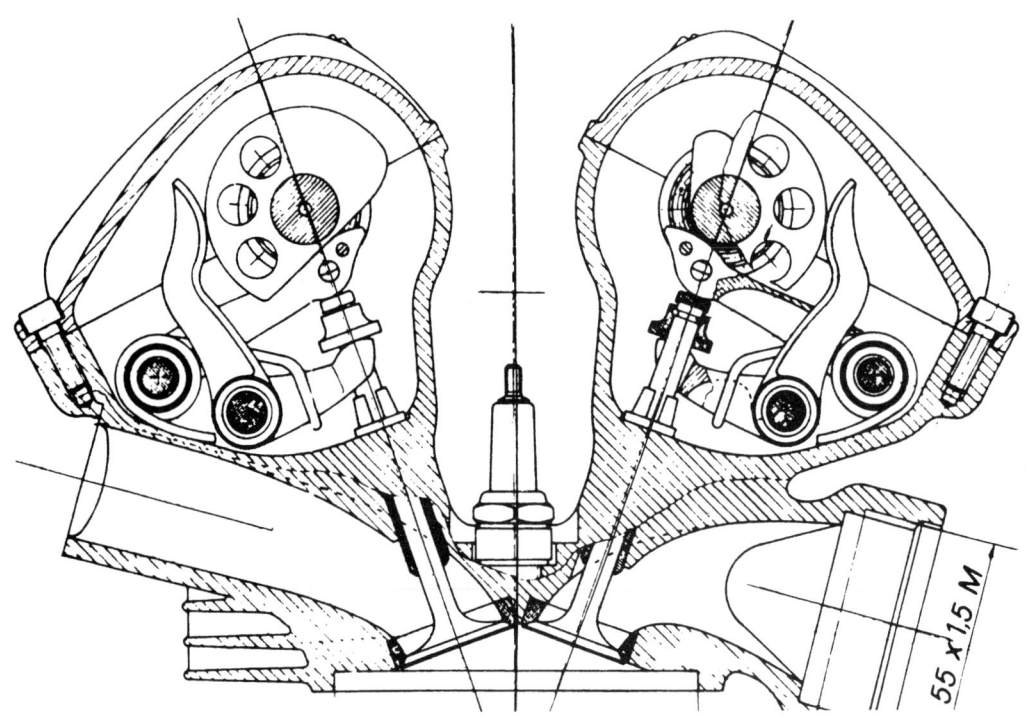

The origins of Ing. Massimo Bordi's dohc V-twin engine came from his graduate thesis about an (air-cooled) Desmo cylinder head. In this layout, the camshafts are directly above the valves acting on finger followers; the closing arms are dog-legged.

1986 French Bol d'Or 24-hour endurance race! The Bol d'Or was proof, if any was needed, of how serious Bordi and his team were in giving their new baby *real* testing – even though the race itself was to end in retirement, caused by a broken gearbox.

FUEL INJECTION

The project, which gained entirely new purpose-built crankcases in early 1987, also saw the engine displacement rise several times before finally selecting 851cc (92 × 64mm). But one feature did remain virtually constant throughout – the use of the Weber-Marelli integrated electronic fuel and injection system, which had originally been used by Ferrari in their Formula 1 racing cars. Bordi, his assistant Luigi Mengoli and veteran Ducati man and former racer Franco Farné, decided on the Weber-Marelli system for a number of sound and well thought-out reasons. In the first place, this particular choice was the most practical; Weber themselves were located near by in Bologna and would therefore be on hand not only to provide the best possible service but also, and perhaps most important of all, to be reached quickly as and when any problems emerged during the project's development phase.

Virtually all the components making up the Weber-Marelli system to be used by Ducati were already fully developed and in series production; for example, the fuel injectors themselves were identical to those found in several Fiat and Lancia cars. This use of mass production items meant that not only were they fully proven, but also relatively inexpensive – had Ducati needed major purpose-built components, then the cost of the whole project would have spiralled upwards. The immediate availability of these mass-produced items was another major factor that enabled the four-valve prototype series

A prototype four-valve engine showing the cylinder head with central spark plug location, cam belts, injectors and dry clutch.

to move from drawing board to production readiness in such a short space of time.

But of course all these advantages would have meant nothing if the system did not suit its new use, or if it was found to be wanting in either reliability or future development potential. As it happened, Bordi and his team did not need to worry: the Weber-Marelli 'open loop' electronic fuel injection was reliable, it did work on two wheels, it was capable of meeting current and future emission regulations, it provided excellent fuel economy without sacrificing power output *and*

Weber-Marelli electronic fuel injection system

Ducati selected the Weber-Marelli 'open loop' electronic fuel injection system, which had already not only seen widespread use in several Lancia and Fiat models, but had also been developed with Ferrari for use in their Formula 1 cars.

This system features a limited number of sensors, and in some respects resembles the type used on Kawasaki's air-cooled GPZ 1100 B2 of the early 1980s. The sensors monitor air temperature and density, coolant temperature, engine revolutions, throttle position and ignition combustion (or detonation). There is no box-like flow meter as used in the Bosch F1 system of the BMW K series motorcycles, nor a lambda probe to enhance fuel injection, often used by the latest automobile ignition systems.

Inside the Weber-Marelli computer memory a number of 'maps' have been encoded, and on the basis of the engine's running conditions, combined with information coming from the sensors, the computer then plots the optimum ignition advance curve as well as the timing of the injectors. Fuel is supplied at a pressure of 43.5psi (3 bar) by an electric pump and is thence squirted directly into the inlet tracts by a pair of injectors for each cylinder, in a phased mode. It should be noted that from the 1989 model year only a single injector has been employed, except in the SP/SPS super sport models and the pure racing machines (both the production Corsa and full-blown factory versions). By comparison, the German Bosch F1 system uses a 'gate' to measure the weight and flow of air entering the engine unit. The system's 'brain' then decides (subject to load, engine speed and other factors) exactly how much fuel the injectors should throw into this measured mass of air for optimum combustion. Although the Bosch system is highly accurate, its gate nonetheless restricts airflow into the engine, and ultimate performance is therefore muted.

Whereas BMW, with their touring-bias machinery, might not be too worried about extracting every last fraction of performance, Ducati were just the opposite, and chief designer Ing. Bordi therefore appreciated the fact that the Weber-Marelli fuel injection, with its 'mapped' system, did not rely on measuring the air flow directly, instead reacting to feedback from the engine.

The basis of the system is what is known as the Alpha angle – the degree of opening of the throttle butterfly varying from 90 degrees, with the throttle closed, to 0 degrees flat out.

Using a dynamometer, Weber's design chief, Aureliano Lionello, connected the dohc, four-valve, 90-degree, liquid-cooled V-twin powerplant to a flow meter and exhaust gas analyser, then tuned the injector system and ignition advance to deliver optimum performance at sixteen different angles of sixteen different rev bands. The resulting mass of data was then plotted into graphs referring to possible operating conditions, using a special computer. Lionello then mapped the Weber system's microchip to conform to the lessons learnt from this information during actual operation.

The system's microprocessor (brain) also corrects for water (or oil) and air temperatures, atmospheric pressure, fuel pressure and changes in battery voltage; choke function and injection timing and duration are also varied subject to the microchip's map. The programming can be varied to improve engine braking, fuel consumption and exhaust emissions.

Any changes to an engine's specification, say for example a different camshaft profile, will usually require a reprogrammed chip. This is partly why a full-blown works racing machine is much more complex to set up than a standard production unit, which is using a stock item.

appeared to have considerable future development potential.

One of the visibly most obvious components of the Weber-Marelli fuel injection system on the four-valve Ducati V-twin series are the truly immense inlet tracts (50mm on the original production 851 series and even larger now), which feed dead straight to the paired inlet valves. In the good (or bad) old days, depending how one views the pre-Cagiva take-over era, the largest choke size Ducati could get away with, even on their works racing motorcycles, was 42mm; if it was any larger, air speed through the carburettor at low rpm was simply not sufficient to pull fuel up from the float bowl quickly and accurately enough. In direct contrast, fuel injection, because of its use of external pressure to push fuel into the engine, suffers none of these glitches.

Bordi and his development team were probably the first major players in the motorcycle word to harness the benefits of a computerized fuel injection and ignition

Ducati mechanics discuss the four-valve machine at Misano on 19 April 1987.

Franco Farné, one of the key figures in the four-valve development story.

Less than two weeks later, on 13 September, the bike was completed, and four days later the machine left Bologna by van destined for the Paul Ricard circuit and its debut in the Bol d'Or.

Of course all this was only possible because of the truly superhuman efforts of Ing. Bordi and his team of Ducati's *reparto sperimentale* (experimental department). Headed by chief technician Franco Farné, the development team not only had to work around the clock to meet such an exacting schedule, but were doing this whilst pushing out the envelope of technology by a considerable degree, combining as they were the ingredients of four-valves-per-cylinder technology and liquid cooling with such well-known Ducati features as the desmodromic valve system and 90-degree V-twin layout. Furthermore, the whole concoction was to be fed by an unfamiliar (to them) sophisticated, computer-controlled fuel injection-cum-ignition system.

ROAD TESTING

Prior to being actually fitted into the chassis the prototype engine had completed over 150 hours on the dyno and, having exceeded the 100bhp/9,500rpm mark with A1 reliability, it was deemed ready for its real-world test.

Following this first outing (albeit one in such trying conditions as on the Bol d'Or), the four-valve engine went back to the design stage before eventually emerging early the following year with a final displacement hike to 851cc (92×64mm). In this form it was not only to win its first race (the 1987 Daytona Battle of the Twins event), but was electronically timed at 165.44mph (266.19km/h) in the same event. This would have made it Daytona's seventh-fastest motorcycle that year had it been allowed to

system to its full potential on what was soon to become a series production motorcycle. And their use of such systems has been one of the major technical innovations in the two wheels world in the last decade.

As an example of just how quickly the new liquid-cooled four-valve engine came about is to recall that in April 1986 there was little more than dimensional blueprints being issued to the relevant foundries and precision workshops. By the beginning of September everything had been manufactured and final construction was started.

The Ducati squad at Misano, 19 April 1987. In the foreground is the two-valve 750 ridden by Raymond Roche that day; in the background, the new four-valve model.

compete in the famous 200-miler. The fact was that it equalled the Superbike-category Yoshimura GSX-R750 Suzuki of eventual 200-miler runner-up Satoshi Tsujimoto, and was only 6mph (9.6km/h) slower than Wayne Rainey's race-winning works VFR 750 Honda V-four. Suddenly everyone in the States was talking the word Ducati, quite something for a country so long accustomed to Japanese domination in the road-racing sphere. Previously Ducatis had always been known as handlers rather than goers in the land of the Big Apple.

Yet, strangely, it was the handling rather than the engine that was to present Ducati with their biggest problems. At Daytona the development bike had been piloted by the 1981 500 Grand Prix champion Marco

Besides those already mentioned, the four-valve development team also consisted of the following specialists: Giuliano Pedretti (engine and electronics), Rugero Nannini (chassis) and Sergio Tibaldi (bodywork).

The definitive production models of the four-valve vee were officially launched towards the end of November. Ducati presented not one but two distinct models, the 851 Strada and 851 Kit, at no less illustrious occasion than the charismatic first day of the biennial Milan Show, the fiftieth such event to be staged.

An 851 series four-valve engine under test in Ducati's experimental department.

Former 500cc world champion Marco Lucchinelli carried out most of the initial track testing with the four-valve engine. He also went on to win the very first World Super Bike race (in 1988, at Donington Park).

'Lucky' Lucchinelli, who reported that whilst pushing hard the front end of the machine displayed a tendency to drift wide. This was, in Lucchinelli's opinion, the cause of a crash later at Misano. The 16in front wheel was later to be cited as a major cause.

Moreover, anyone looking for an all-new aluminium chassis was destined to be disappointed, as Ducati chose to remain faithful to the tubular steel chrome-molybdenum type pioneered on the Pantah series. The ladder-and-lattice style frame broadly resembled the structure used on the earlier air-cooled two-valve TTF2 and TTF1 racers campaigned in the first half of the 1980s.

3　The 851

When Ducati's epitaph is finally written, the numbers 851 must surely appear in bold print, so significant was this motorcycle series in the transformation of the marque from one catering purely for the loyal enthusiast to one of a truly international broad appeal as it is today. Headlines such as 'Stunner', 'A Slice of Marco' and 'Magic at a Price' were typical of the press reaction following the launch of the production 851 four-valve models at the 1987 Milan Show.

But it was to be some six months before Ducati officially allowed the press to *ride* the newcomers at Misano race circuit, in late May 1988. This coincided with the bikes being distributed to dealers; the first customers taking delivery in June. As the series was so new, Ducati opted to build a total of

The public debut of the new 851 came at the Milan Show in November 1987. Production began early the following year.

Specially cutaway engine assembly on the company's stand at the 1987 Milan Show reveals many of the design's features.

just 500 851s during 1988 – 300 Stradas and 200 Kit versions. The latter was offered so that the company would reach the minimum number needed to homologate the type for WSB (World Super Bike) racing.

Motor Cycle News, in their 1 June 1988 issue, made a pretty accurate statement, saying: 'The 851 is a radical departure on some respects, but it's still chock full of traditional Ducati values'. Reporter Chris Dobbs went on to say:

A 90-degree V-twin, an engine layout Ducati have made their own over the years, complete with desmodromic valve gear is housed in a tubular steel frame similar to the 750F1 and Pantahs. No surprises there! But this bike has a liquid-cooled engine, four valves per cylinder, and most significantly fuel injection. Fitting Weber-Marelli

fuel injection has enabled Ducati to leapfrog the Japanese in the technology stakes, extracting enough power from the twin (101bhp) to put it on par with Jap fours, and clean up engine response and emissions!

Although the racing department already knew that 17in wheels were better than 16in, Bordi and his team still chose to fit 16in on the Strada version of the 1988 851, and this and the use of bimetal floating 280mm discs with four-piston Brembo P4 32B calipers at the front in place of 320mm full floating assemblies on Lucchinelli's bike were the two main failings. A 260mm single solid disc was fitted at the rear, with a double piston P2 T08N caliper.

The Strada had a distinct tendency to 'pick up' a lot in corners whilst on the brakes; in other words it would sit up as soon as the brakes were applied. This was not only unnerving but it also forced the rider into a more heavy-handed approach than with 17 or 18in wheels. The Kit version was fitted with 17in Marvics for the latest slicks, but at this stage in its development the 851 was not as good as later models. To quote one tester during 1988, 'You had to push it hard through the bends to get the tyres to work'.

Except for its larger-diameter wheels and also open exhausts, lack of indicators and mirrors – plus the use of racing slicks instead of treaded tyres – the Kit version *appeared* surprisingly similar to the Strada. This similarity was heightened by the same red, white and green colour scheme – soon known as the Tricolore (three colours).

STRADA AND KIT VERSIONS

Mechanically, there were notable differences between the two versions. For the Strada, factory sources claimed 100.5bhp at 9,250rpm (at the crankshaft), whereas the

The more exclusive, faster and more expensive Kit version.

Unofficially known as the Tricolore (three colour) due to its red, white and green paint job, the Strada (seen here) and Kit (above) were only offered for the 1988 model year.

Kit put out 119bhp at 10,000rpm (again at the crank), with a maximum rpm limit of 9,500 and 10,500rpm respectively.

To achieve the higher output the Kit came with different camshafts, a race exhaust, higher compression pistons (10.6:1), nimonic steel valves, a dry clutch (the Strada had a wet assembly) and a different Eprom computer chip. The Kit also had closer ratio gears from third to top on the six-speed box. Unlike the Strada the hotter version did not run out of steam at 9,500rpm, instead revving strongly to the 10,500rpm red line. It also had a new subframe, no starter, a lightened flywheel and generator – and less weight, 330lb (150kg), compared to the 340lb (155kg) of the Strada.

Both variants of the 1988 851 production series had the same basic format with regard to the engine castings, with belt-driven double overhead camshafts (if not the cam profile themselves); aluminium alloy cylinder barrels with silicon carbide inner coating; forged slipper pistons (but of different ratios); one-piece steel crankshaft, and double-webbed H-section Pankl racing-strength connecting rods. Made in Austria, these last items were machined from solid billet with split plain bearing big-ends. The crankcase closely followed those of the earlier two-valves-per-cylinder Pantah engine series with the swinging arm pivot running through them to reduce the machine's wheelbase. The cases were to prove one of the four-valvers' main weaknesses, certainly if highly tuned or raced. Again the external cartridge oil filter (with a sump capacity of 4 litres) and front-mounted electric sporter motor followed Pantah practice; as did the oil sight glass located on the offside of the outer engine case.

Chassis-wise, except for the already mentioned wheels, the 1988 851 Strada and Kit were virtually identical. The suspension on both was identical. This meant a pair of 41.7mm stanchions up front for the Marzocchi MIR, 100mm stroke telescopic forks, while at the rear there was the luxury of a vertically mounted monoshock with full rising rate (unlike on the two-valve Ducatis of the same period like the F1 and Paso, which had to make do with the vastly inferior and outmoded cantilever rear end). The monoshock used was a Marzocchi Supermono with 50mm of travel. And apart from the usual pre-load and rebound adjustment, there was an extremely useful snail-cam for adjusting the monoshock linkage ratios. All this was to give the 851 a level of comfort undreamed of on previous Ducati V-twins. The Kit had a specially braced swinging arm, and both assemblies were in extruded aluminium.

The fuel capacity of the Strada and Kit *was* different – the former being 22 litres, the latter 21 litres. But both sizes were manufactured in aluminium alloy.

The majority of the electrics, which *Bike* (September 1988) described as being 'enough to rewire the average house', were crammed, with the 12 volt, 16 amp hour battery, into the space beneath the seat hump, and were also of a much higher standard than on previous Dukes. Of course much of this was due to the Weber-Marelli electronic fuel injection

Control layout of the 1988 851 Kit model. Note lack of speedometer.

and ignition system. *Bike* had this to say: 'a strange noise that sounds like a guinea pig being put painfully to death [how come they knew this particular noise, one asks?] assails your senses from under the tank. Animal lovers will be relieved to learn that this is merely the fuel injection system's fuel pump performing its ritual pre-start work out!'

The Strada cost £10,995 and the Kit £12,995 in 1988. Taking into account inflation since then, both bikes seem hyperexpensive, certainly *more* expensive than their modern-day counterparts ... but of course Ducati production costs have dropped in comparison to the late 1980s owing to vastly increased production, if nothing else. But it is worth noting that the Kit version did come with a comprehensive spares package (hence the Kit label). However, in practice many bikes were sold without the spares, either for a lower price, or, in some cases, by unscrupulous dealers.

As for performance, the Strada was claimed to be good for 'over 140mph [225km/h]'. But *Bike* only achieved a best one way of 133.9mph (215.4km/h) in their September 1988 test. The same magazine also put the same bike on the dyno and achieved 89.1bhp at 8,500rpm. But these were 'real world' figures taken at the rear wheel, not the crankshaft. *Bike* also carried out their Strada dyno tests with airbox and filter in place; once these had been removed the figure went up to 95bhp.

The *Bike* tester brought to the public's attention the efficiency of the aerodynamics of the Strada and the fact that this was 'as important as horsepower'. Going on to say 'whatever angle you find yourself at [referring to the mirror, which was only of any use in a crouched racing stance!] you can't fail to notice the protection offered by the 851's fairing. For all its apparent racer styling it manages to keep all but boot and shoulder tips protected from airborne nasties. Quite

The author (left) with David Woolsey, the first British rider to race an 851 Kit, at Snetterton in June 1988.

an unexpected bonus on one so apparently single in purpose!'

If the Strada was not as fast as it purported to be, the Kit certainly was, with another magazine (*Performance Bikes*) electronically achieving 159.7mph (256.9km/h)! But of course this was with the advantage not just of extra tuning, but an exhaust system that was illegal for street use.

In all, the initial 851 built for the 1988 model year was more good than bad. The only really negative aspects were the handling (on the Strada, with its 16in wheels, in particular), braking (at least compared to what followed), the mirrors, minor electrical and fuel injection glitches and a dealer network to whom modern technology was new in itself, which caused many unnecessary problems.

Two 851 Kits were raced at The Cock of the North race meeting at Olivers Mount, Scarborough on the 1/2 June 1988. Even with 17in Marvic wheels, as seen here, the handling left something to be desired. Neither machine finished in the results.

(Below) *Besides a new red bodywork/white frame and wheels paint finish, the 1989 model year saw several revisions to the production 851 series. These resulted in not only a lower price, but also a superior motorcycle. Effectively the old Strada became the Monoposto (single seat), whilst the Kit was uprated into the pure racing Corsa model.*

It should also be remembered that in Britain the launch of the 851 was handled by no less than *four* importers: Moto Cinelli in Northampton, Sports Motorcycles in Bollington, Cheshire, Three Cross in Dorset and Moto Vecchia in Dorking, Surrey. In the United States, by contrast, Cagiva themselves were struggling to set up an in-house funded distribution network, which was then very much in its infancy.

THE 1989 MODEL YEAR

For the 1989 model year Ducati set out to cure the majority of the problems experienced with the initial year's bikes.

To start with, the Strada and Kit names were axed, as was the Tricolore paint scheme. Cost was also a major issue and the 1989 bike, officially known as the 851 Superbike '89, was considerably cheaper to buy. Here Ducati took something of a gamble. To sell the machine at a cheaper price

they had to build far more bikes (something like 4,000 bikes in total).

Also known as the Monoposto (single seat), the new 851 came with 17in wheels as standard, modified suspension settings, with the front fork stroke reduced from 100 to 95mm, and the Marzocchi single shock updated by the new Duoshock with 65mm instead of the 50mm stroke specified for the previous year!

These changes, together with other, more minor ones to the chassis, resulted in considerable overall improvement.

Other important differences were to be found in the braking system, with a change to the larger 320mm fully floating discs at the front, whilst at the rear the disc diameter was reduced to 245mm. These particular changes followed World Super Bike experience.

More minor changes included a slight restyling of the bodywork, which was now all red, mirrors mounted on stalks instead of flush fitting, as had been the case on the 1988 Strada, and a single injector per cylinder. The frame colour was now white (in 1988 it had been silver), as were the cast alloy three-spoke wheels. To reduce the cost further the Pankl connecting rods were now only specified for the new Lucchinelli Replica (888cc) over-the-counter racer, which had effectively replaced the previous years Kit version. Details of the customer racer's are given in Chapter 4.

Official factory performance figures for the new single-model street 851 were 105bhp (at the crank) and 149mph (240km/h) top speed.

(Above) *The '851' logo on the seat of an Italian-registered 1989 851 Monoposto.*

The finishing touches are carried out by factory workers to 1989 model 851 Monopostos, in April that year.

Stacking finished crankcases at the factory in 1989. Note the conveyor-type line of cases in the upper rear of the picture.

(Below) A 1989 851 Monoposto with the seat, tank and fairing lower panels removed. Note the battery location, radiator, steel trellis frame and separate rear subframe in much smaller diameter tubing. The swinging arm is aluminium, the suspension by Marzocchi.

The author's Italian friend Gerolamo Bettoni pictured with one of the very first 851 Monoposto models, in spring 1989.

To confuse things Ducati also launched, with little publicity at the time, the SP1 (Sport Production Number 1). Initially intended purely for the Italian sports machine racing formula events, these bikes were to find instant favour with cash-rich collectors/investors/arch-enthusiasts, and Ducati were later to exploit this with a whole series of similar limited edition versions, offered with an official silver numbering plate (usually found on the machine's top yoke, or triple clamp in the USA). But because the SP1 and later versions were actually of the larger 888cc (96×64mm) their story is charted in Chapter 5.

1990 TO 1992

The 1990 model year saw the arrival of the 851 Biposto (dual seat), with styling largely the same as on the 851 Monoposto, except for the seating arrangements. On the Biposto (thereafter often shortened simply to BP), a pillion pad sat atop the rear seat hump and folding pillion footrests were provided as part of the machine's specification.

As with the previous year's Monoposto, the standard strength, less expensive conrods were also specified. There was also Marzocchi suspension both front and rear.

For 1991 the 851 Biposto changed to inverted (upside-down) Japanese-made Showa front forks and a Swedish Öhlins rear shock. The styling remained as before, but the fuel tank shape was modified. There was also a decal proclaiming Ducati's first WSB championship (Raymond Roche had won the previous year). A technical change appeared in the increased capacity of both the front brake and clutch master cylinder reservoirs.

For the 1992 model year the mainstream 851 (the Biposto) was restyled. This largely centred around the rear seat section, which now incorporated improved pillion comfort (probably Ducati were worried about the effects their top-selling Superbike was having on the divorce rates!), with foldaway

(Opposite page) See if you can tell the differences between these 1990 and 1991 851 Biposto (dual seat) models! The 1990 has black round mirrors (red on the 1991 bike), a larger front mudguard, conventional Marzocchi forks (inverted Showa forks on 1991 machine) and other smaller, less noticeable differences.

grab rails. The material of the fuel tank was changed from alloy to steel. Incidentally, the SP4 (still 888cc) which superseded the SP3, now also found itself with a steel rather than aluminium fuel tank. And an entirely new model, the SP5 (again 888cc) arrived – *refer to* Chapter 5.

By the end of 1992 the 851 as a motorcycle, both in name and cubic capacity, had been axed. In its place for the 1993 model year (which effectively now began when workers returned from their annual holidays at the end of August) came the 888 Strada (the Biposto). But at least in styling and much of its technical genes the 851 lived on. Only with the major redesign that came a year later and resulted in the superb 916 did things really take a quantum leap forward.

But Ducati, their importers and their worldwide fans have much to thank the 851 for: without it none of the modern miracle would have happened.

The late Ayrton Senna with an 851 Biposto in 1992. Senna was a close friend of the Castiglioni family, the owners of the Ducati name.

(Above) *Ducati first offered a 'customer' racer in 1988. This was known as the Lucchinelli Replica. It, like the Corsa that replaced it in 1989, used an 888cc (94 × 64mm) engine that revved to 11,000rpm, was fitted with 17in Marvic wheels and twin 300mm front discs/single 260mm rear disc brakes. Other features included a braced aluminium swinging arm, Marzocchi front forks and a dry weight of less than 353lb (160kg).*

(Left) *This is the actual prototype Corsa, seen whilst under test early in 1989. It was clearly based on the factory models of the period – but was not quite so quick!*

4 Customer Racers

Running in tandem with Ducati's success in World Super Bike racing has come a series of over-the-counter 'customer' racers.

The 1988 851 Kit should be considered the first of these models (*see* Chapter 3). This was very much a homologation 'special' to allow Ducati the chance to take part in the new World Super Bike (WSB) series, which began that year. However, this first effort at building a 'customer' version of Ducati's new four-valves-per-cylinder V-twin was not particularly effective as a racing machine. The first real 851 series racer did not in fact enter production until the 1989 model year.

Whereas the 851 Kit was what it said – 851cc (92 × 64mm) – the 1989 bike, known as the Lucchinelli Replica, used the larger 888cc (96 × 64mm) of the then current works racers. Only twenty-nine of these machines were built, and in Britain the price was around £18,000. Besides the bigger engine displacement and handbuilt assembly, the Lucchinelli Replica had carbon-fibre bodywork (including the fairing), a well as Marzocchi front forks and lightweight Marvic wheels. Even performance, although considerably improved over the previous year's 851 Kit, still wasn't really any great shakes.

For 1990 the Corsa was updated with improved suspension (using inverted forks for the first time at the front), less weight (down from 159 to 155kg) and revised braking – the twin front discs being increased in diameter to 320mm, whilst the single rear decreased to 210mm. Further weight reduction and decrease in rear brake disc diameter to 190mm came from 1991 onwards. The Corsa shown here is a 1992 model.

The Corsa in 888cc guise was to remain in production from 1989 through to the 1993 model year. But that is not to say it didn't change: in fact there were yearly updates. For example, the 1991 version, the specification of which was released in September 1990, is quite typical; it had the following changes:

Carbon-fibre air intake
Carbon-fibre instrument panel/half fairing
Marvic 3.75/17 6/17 wheels
New front mudguard
Gold D34/30 Brembo calipers
Rear 190mm disc (replacing a 210mm component)
New (carbon-fibre) airbox
Carbon-fibre fuel tank
Carbon-fibre silencer brackets
Higher silencers
Uprated water radiator
New (lightened) trimming
New inlet bellmouths for injectors
Showa steering damper
Modified front suspension with increased adjustment
Modified rear suspension shock absorber with increased adjustment
Weight reduction of around 17¼lb (8kg)
Increased power output at the rear wheel to a claimed 128bhp @ 11,000rpm

For the 1992 model year there were another batch of changes, although the power output at 128bhp (rear wheel) remained unchanged:

New exhaust assembly including both pipes and mufflers
New wheels (including cush drive at rear)
New coolant circuit, including radiator
Rear disc diameter reduced to 190mm
Smaller battery and carbon-fibre support
Smaller fuel pump
Magnesium front fork top yoke
New front fork legs
Exhaust camshafts
Connecting rod with lubricating hole to match piston
Lighter piston of a new forging material
Gudgeon pin diameter changed to 21mm
Gearbox with revised ratios
Light alloy timing belt tensioners
With other lightening details some 11lb (5kg) was saved, reducing dry weight to 330lb (150kg), including oil and water, but not fuel

For the 1993 model year there were few significant changes, except for an improved clutch, an electronic (instead of mechanical) tachometer, revised gearchange and minor

By 1992 the word had spread around that Ducati had a competitive racer, not simply for the official works WSB squad, but privateers too. Orders for the Corsa were by now outstripping supply, with only the top riders/teams being able to purchase one. In the UK one of the leading race teams of the period was Oxford Products, headed by Malcolm Hammond; one of their riders in 1992 (and 1993) was Joey Dunlop's younger brother, Robert.

(Right) *Another British rider to make an impact on the home circuits that year aboard one of the booming 888 Corsas was a certain Carl Fogarty, seen here in winning form at the British Supercup meeting at Donington Park in May 1992. After some brilliant rides that year he was signed by the factory for the 1993 season.*

(Left) *Yet another Brit was the young Michael Rutter (son of four-times Ducati world champion, Tony). Michael is seen here at Brands Hatch with model Yasmin Le Bon in September 1992. His Moto Cinelli-backed machine was actually an 888 SPS tuned to Corsa specification.*

(Above) *Michael Rutter in vivid action on the Moto Cinelli Corsa-spec 888 SPS on his way to victory during the summer of 1992.*

Michael Rutter's machine on display at the Italian Motorcycle Owners Club weekend, Cadwell Park, in July 1992.

For 1993 the 888 Corsa was reduced in weight once more, this time down to 326lb (148kg). The styling of both the seat and the tank was changed, whilst the exhaust was raised. The wheel supplier was also swapped from Marvic to Marchesini.

Carl Fogarty (4) and Robert Dunlop (1) on their 888 Corsas await the start of the 1993 North West 200. Number 3 is Honda works star Joey Dunlop.

Carl Fogarty on the Moto Cinelli 888 Corsa during the 1993 North West 200. Foggy was provided with this bike for non-world championship meetings via the factory, through its importers, Moto Cinelli.

(Below) Foggy hurls the Moto Cinelli 888 Corsa into vivid cornering action during the North West 200, May 1993. Note those kerb stones!

alterations to the injector/ignition CPU and frame – plus new graphics.

THE 1994 MODEL YEAR

But for 1994 the Corsa's engine was considerably improved, even though the running gear remained the old 851/888 series rather than the new-for-1994 916 (*see* right).

Engine

926cc (96 × 64mm)
Improved gear engagement
Reinforced crankcase
Titanium connecting rods
Larger 37mm inlet valves
New oil-bleed system
Lighter moving parts

Frame

Various lightening details
Deletion of anti-hopping rear rake rod
Mercury switch for cut-out in case of accident
Öhlins front fork, rear shock and steering damper
Larger brake calipers
Narrow-face front brake discs
Thinner rear brake disc
Lighter five-spoke Marvic magnesium wheels
New tyres:
Front 12/60 17SC 1275 Michelin slick
Rear 18/67 SC 1866 Michelin slick
Optimized airbox
Oil bleed tank
Exhaust system
Seat body

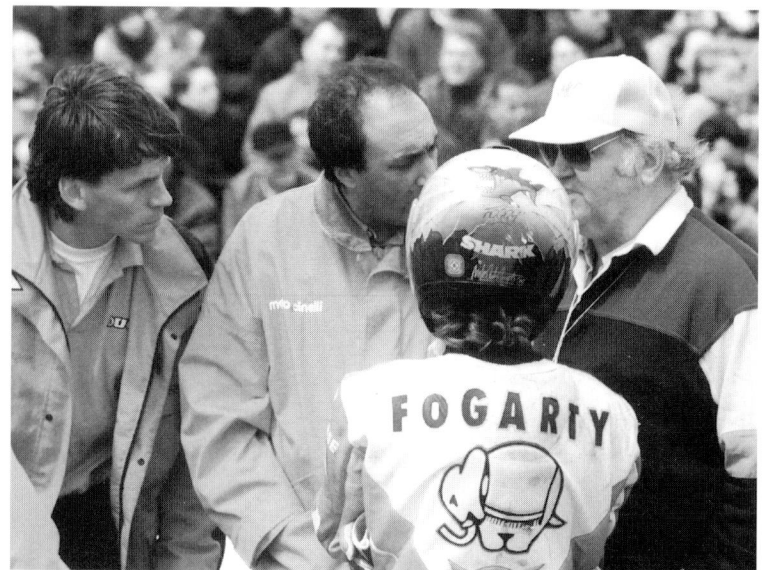

The Moto Cinelli team at the 1993 North West 200 included Foggy, his mechanic Anthony 'Slick' Bass (far left), Moto Cinelli boss Hoss Elm (centre), and Moto Cinelli manager Malcolm Wheeler (not in picture). Also in the frame is ACU official and former racer Bill Smith (right).

(Below) In 1994, Matt Llewellyn surprised many observers by winning several of the early British Championship rounds on a new 926cc Corsa provided by long-time sponsors, Meakin Racing.

Strangely, Ducati did not sell the Corsa with the new 916 style in 1994. Instead they upped the capacity to 926cc, whilst keeping the 888-type running gear. Also note the new wheel design, with five spokes instead of three.

THE 1995 MODEL YEAR

For the 1995 model year the Corsa was based around the new 916 series, not the previous 851/888 model range. Not only this, but once again the engine displacement was given a hike upwards.

Specification	
Engine displacement	955cc
Bore	96mm
Stroke	66mm
Max. rpm	11,500
Inlet opens	BTDC 53
Inlet closes	ABDC 71
Exhaust opens	BBDC 71
Exhaust closes	ATDC 45
Primary drive gearing	15/37
Dry weight	320lb (145kg)

THE 1996 MODEL YEAR

For 1996 the Corsa became the 916 Racing. Differences from the 1995 model Corsa were:

Engine

Inlet camshaft as factory 1995 engine
Exhaust system 52mm diameter
Clutch with back torque limiter (again as on 1995 factory bikes)
Oil pump with enclosed relief valve
Timing belts (Kevlar)

Frame

Dry weight 352lb (160kg), as per 1996 Super Bike rules
Front fork now with top-out spring
Rear shock with aluminium casing and fast pre-load adjuster
Thicker front brake discs
Deletion of air vents on rear seat section

Although badged as a 916, the 1998 Corsa was in fact 996cc (98 × 66mm). The new 916 style Corsa had debuted in the 1995 model year as a 955 (96 × 66mm). The 996cc arrived for the 1997 model year.

THE 1997 MODEL YEAR

For the 1997 model year another series of modifications were introduced:

Engine displacement — 996cc
Bore and stroke — 98 × 66mm
Primary drive — 32/59
Pressure regulator — 5 bar
Adjustable offset fork yokes (triple clamps in the USA)
Enlarged front brake discs
Larger oil radiator
Airbox with larger capacity
Front fairing with larger air intake duct
Exhaust system — 54mm bore
New rear wheel hub assembly
Improved half handlebar (clip-on) fixing
Non-painted fairing

THE 1998 MODEL YEAR

Another year of development by the factory machines was to lead to the annual improvement of the 916 Racing customer model. The full list for the 1998 version was as follows:

Lighter piston and connecting rod
Crankshaft: balancing factor revised to suit the new piston/con-rod assembly, coupling spline for sprocket
Primary drive sprocket manufactured from improved material and with coupling spline
Improved crankshaft shimming
New inlet manifolds
New oil seal at crankshaft oil inlet
Timing belt rollers with larger rims
Smoother gearchange control thanks to new selector drum
Magnesium swinging arm
Throttle body for injectors, 60mm
24-litre (5.3imp. gal) fuel tank
Front forks with same axle lugs as 1997 factory bike
Front brake disc diameter of 290mm supplied as standard
Waterproof injection control unit cover
Larger capacity coolant radiator
Hydraulic adjustment for rear suspension single-shock pre-load
TIG-welded frame in $25CrMo_4$, thickness 1.5mm
Lighter seat subframe

5 The 888

The 888cc (96 × 64mm) engine size was pioneered on works prototype racing machines and then on the factory's customer racing model (sold as the Lucchinelli Replica) during the first year of World Super Bike (WSB) competition in 1988 (*see* Chapters 4 and 8). To confuse the issue even further, there was also a tiny batch of the SP1 (Sport Production No 1) 851s, using the 888cc engine displacement, for Italian sport machine racing. Well, that was the SP1's intended use, but, as the factory was to discover time over time, the majority of these limited production machines were snapped up by cash-rich collectors for storage and ride-outs on dry summer days. For most of its life the 888cc power unit was used in motorcycles marketed under the 851 label.

The 1990 model year saw the arrival of the SP2, which had Swedish Öhlins upside-down forks and a rear shock from the same source.

For the 1991 model year the stock 851 (*see* Chapter 3) also gained upside-down (inverted) forks, but of Showa manufacture, with Öhlins rear shock. That same year the SP3 replaced the SP2. Differences between the models included a higher-level exhaust and an increase in reservoir capacity of both front brake and clutch master cylinders (the latter improvements also found their way into the standard 851cc models). And, in line with the stock 851 series, the tank shape was altered.

For the 1992 model year the base-model 851 was restyled and the fuel tank material was changed from alloy to steel. The SP4

The SPS of 1992 was the ultimate Ducati V-twin, if the pure racing Corsa and factory one-off models are discounted, prior to the debut of the 916 series in 1994. Only built that year, the 888 SPS featured a Corsa specification engine and extra carbon-fibre. Only a hundred were constructed, and it was a pukka race bike in everything but name.

An 888 SPS with the fairing panels removed to show the technical details usually hidden from view.

replaced the SP3, and this too had the steel fuel tank, together with another change to the exhaust system, which provided yet more ground clearance.

A new model entirely was the SPS, of which only 100 were ever built. Styling was identical to the SP4, but with carbon-fibre silencers (mufflers), carbon-fibre fuel tank and a 1991-specification Corsa (racing) engine. In truth, the SPS was virtually a full race bike and came with a race radiator unit, which had no cooling fan.

For 1993 the 851 was finally discontinued, being replaced by the 888 Strada (Biposto). The SP5 (also a 1993 model) utilized the same engine as the SPS, including the use of two injectors per cylinder instead of only one, as used on the less highly tuned series production models. Also, as with the SPS, the SP5 came with carbon-fibre

---

The 888 SP5 (1993)

Engine	Liquid-cooled, dohc, four-valves-per-cylinder, 90-degree V-twin, belt-driven overhead camshafts
Bore and stroke	94 × 64mm
Displacement	888cc
Compression ratio	11.5:1
Max. power (at crank)	118bhp
Lubrication	Forced feed gear pump, with oil cooler
Ignition	Electronic IAW type
Fuel system	Weber-Marelli electronic indirect type, 2 injectors per cylinder
Primary drive	Straight cut gears (crank 31 teeth, clutch 62)
Final drive	Chain DID 520 ERV2 (gearbox sprocket 15 teeth, rear wheel 36 teeth)
Gearbox	6 speeds, straight cut gears
Clutch	Multi-plate, 8+8 with 16 friction surfaces
Frame	Lattice type, round steel 25 chrome-molybdenum$_4$
Front suspension	Showa inverted telescopic fork with 41mm stanchion diameter, fully adjustable. Travel 120mm
Rear suspension	Öhlins DU 8071 adjustable oleopneumatic monoshock. Shock travel 65mm
Front brake	Twin 320mm fully floating Brembo brake discs, 4-piston calipers
Rear brake	Single 245mm disc, 2-piston caliper
Wheels	3-spoke light alloy
Front Tyre	120/70 ZR 17in
Rear Tyre	180/55 ZR 17in
Valve sizes	Inlet 37mm, exhaust 31mm
Valve timing	Inlet opens 53 BTDC/closes 71 ABDC
	Exhaust opens 72 BBDC/closes 42 ATDC
Wheelbase	56in (1,430mm)
Width	26in (670mm)
Seat height	30in (760mm)
Ground clearance	6in (150mm)
Fuel tank capacity	19 litres (4.18imp. gal)
Dry weight	414lb (205kg)
Maximum speed	161.5mph (259.9km/h)

(Opposite, above) *The SP series begin in 1989. All used 888cc (94 × 64mm) displacement. This is the SP2 of 1990, even though at this time the factory still put 851 stickers on it!*

(Opposite, below) *The 851 logo again, but in reality the SP3 of 1991 was 888cc. Except for higher exhaust and longer clutch and brake cylinders, it was much as the SP2.*

(Right) *For 1992 the SP3 became the SP4, the main change being a steel fuel tank instead of an aluminium one. This example has the SPS carbon-fibre end cons. The Dunlop stickers are non-standard.*

(Below) *The final 'hot' model in the 888 series was the SP5 of 1993. This came with carbon-fibre end cans (mufflers) as standard; it had the same engine as the SPS, including the two fuel injectors per cylinder.*

A totally stock 1993 888 Strada, featuring the new graphics introduced that year. Because of delays with production of the new 916 model, it continued to be listed into 1994. The owner of this bike is Roy Fuller.

Showa's inverted forks, Brembo goldline four-piston calipers and floating discs mark the 1993 888 Strada.

American enthusiast John Allard with his 888. To quote: 'Enjoying an idyllic summer's day on one of the many roads that criss-cross the pleasant plains of Damascus'.

silencers, but the fuel tank was of steel construction. The capacity of all these models remained at 888cc, even though the pukka works racing bikes campaigned by official factory riders had now been upped to 926cc (*see* Chapter 8).

The new 916 did not enter production until late spring of 1994, thus the yearly batch of Corsa over-the-counter racing models still employed 888-type cycle parts for that model year, but with the larger 926cc displacement (*see* Chapter 4). Meanwhile the 888 series standard production models remained on the factory listings for the early months of 1994. All this is very confusing when you consider the annual changeover usually takes place the previous autumn. But, as is related in Chapter 9, Ducati's owners, Cagiva, were in deep financial trouble,

which first spilled over in the delayed launch of the 888's replacement the 916.

888cc Production Chart

Model	Year
Lucchinelli Replica (racer)	1988
Corsa 888 (racer)	1989–93
SP1	1989
SP2	1990
SP3	1991
SP4	1992
SPS	1992
888 Strada	1993
888 SP5	1993

It is important to realize that several of the models referred to above were marketed as 851s even though the engine displacement was actually 888cc.

Dedicated Sussex Ducati enthusiast Geoff Palmer with his 1992 888 SPS and his 1995 916 SP. Geoff also owns a 1979 Mike Hailwood Replica bevel V-twin and is currently restoring a 1974 250 Desmo single.

Supermono

Without a shadow of a doubt the racing-only Supermono Ducati has to be one of the world's most technically advanced motorcycles – and one of the most stunningly beautiful too. Furthermore, it owed its existence to the new breed of four-valves-per-cylinder V-twins, the 888 series in particular.

Production of this limited edition handbuilt masterpiece began in the summer of 1993, with *Superbike* calling it the 'Red Dwarf', before going on to say: 'we ride the most sophisticated single in the known universe … 75hp, 11,000rpm, 120kg, 146mph'. It was certainly not like any other 'thumper'.

Since Ducati had last built one of their legendary classic bevel singles, in 1974, Ing. Fabio Taglioni had retired and his place as chief designer had been filled by the much younger Massimo Bordi; Ducati also had new owners in the shape of Cagiva, and this was the era of the eight-valve (four per cylinder), fuel-injected, liquid-cooled, dohc V-twin, which had a virtual stranglehold on the WSB (World Super Bike) crown.

Ing. Bordi had first tested his *doppia bielletta* (double con-rod) Supermono engine on the bench during the winter of 1990. This initial prototype had a displacement of 487cc (95.6 × 68mm) with tests revealing 62.5bhp at 10,500 rpm. Next came a 502cc (95.6 × 70mm) version, with power rising to 70bhp, before Bordi and his team finally settled on 549cc (100 × 70mm) as the definitive layout. The power was now up to 75bhp (measured at the gearbox). A pre-production prototype was displayed to the public at the Cologne Show in October 1992.

The second con-rod was in place of a conventional balance shaft, but it was claimed by Bordi to be: 'more compact, and doesn't need any gears of chains to drive it, with their attendant power losses!' All the pivot points were pressure lubricated; and it gave perfect primary balance, as well as eliminating secondary inertia, since it acted directly on the crankshaft.

Much of the Supermono's engine design followed 888 (and of course 851) practice, including Weber-Marelli fuel injection, six-speed gearbox and dry clutch.

Cutaway of Supermono engine, showing its unique doppia bielletta *(double con-rod). The second rod acts as a balancing device.*

A factory development Supermono racer at the Italian championship meeting, Misano, 14 March 1993, with works mechanic Giorgio Grimandi.

(Below) A Supermono on the Ducati stand at the Cologne Show, September 1994. Designed by Massimo Bordi, the technology of this hi-tech single leaned heavily on the 888 V-twin.

Supermono (*continued*)

If the engine was Bordi's creation, the chassis was very much the work of Claudio Domenicali. The tubular steel chassis was manufactured at the Cagiva factory in Varese from a new high-resistance material coded ALS 500, which provided the same stiffness as the more familiar 25 chrome molybdenum$_4$, but at a lower cost.

The Bologna-based Verlicchi concern built the aluminium swinging arm; which pivoted on the crankcases like on all the belt-driven Ducati V-twins. The Swedish suspension specialists Öhlins were responsible for both the inverted front forks and single rear shock.

The third man in the creation of the Supermono was the South African stylist Pierre Terblanche, who was responsible for the model's curvaceous lines.

The Supermono's big advantage was that, unlike the vast majority of its rivals, it had overall ability. Its 75bhp and a weight of 272lb (123.5kg) half-dry was only average. But it was the most complete motorcycle in its class. Racing journalist Alan Cathcart summed it up when he said:

> Being designed as a piece, rather than a modified engine shoehorned into a purpose-built race chassis, it offers a superbly responsive, high-revving engine, with the sophistication of fuel injection helping to deliver a totally linear power curve with the engine tractable from as low as 4,000rpm, pulling up to the 11,000rpm redline without a hiccup – or any vibration.

Production got underway with a batch of thirty machines in the spring of 1993 – which in practice saw delivery being spread over months rather than days.

A Series 2 Supermono, of which some forty-five to fifty examples were constructed from late 1994 onwards, was known as the '102'. This was in reference to its 102mm bore size, giving a new engine displacement of 572cc. This not only provided more top-end speed, but, more importantly, increased drive out of corners, thanks to increased torque figures. Owners of the Series 1 machines can purchase a kit to convert their engine to the later specification.

South African Gary Turner racing the Dutch Pro Carbon 572cc Series 2 Supermono during 1996.

6 The 916

When Ducati launched the new 916 onto the market in 1994 there was simply nothing to touch it. To many enthusiasts around the world it was not merely the latest superbike, but *the* superbike – the best there had ever been. Not just because of its performance, handling and braking, but also its style and charisma. The choice of a Ferrari-red colour scheme only added to the overall effect, as did the 'pillar box' twin-headlamp fairing, hi-level aluminium (Termignoni carbon-fibre on the SP/SPS versions) silencers, single-sided swinging arm and the magical, deep-throated, booming exhaust note.

When the 916 was first seen in public towards the end of 1993 it caused a sensation with its entirely new styling; and in all-round ability it challenged anything on the street.

Massimo Tamburini

Massimo Tamburini has been labelled as one of the greatest motorcycle designers of the late twentieth century – and with good cause. This is, after all, the man who not only helped form the Bimota marque back in the early 1970s, but thereafter was responsible for a truly vast list of motorcycles for both road and track.

In 1983 Tamburini quit Bimota following a disagreement with one of the other members of the founding trio, Giuseppe Morri. This argument centred around Tamburini's view that Bimota was too small an outfit to be designing its own engine; Morri did not agree ... Events have proved Tamburini right – just look at the financial cost Bimota incurred with their 500 V Due (a V-twin two-stroke initially developed for an ill-fated foray in 500cc GP racing and then converted for street use). The debacle almost crippled Bimota with its vast development costs and ultimate failure, which has spanned most of the 1990s since development began!

Born in 1942, Tamburini was thirty years of age when Bimota was founded in 1972. He joined Cagiva in time to pen the Ducati Paso, which made its public debut at the Milan Show in December 1985. Another notable early design for his new employees, the Castiglioni brothers, was the Cagiva Freccia (Arrow), a single-cylinder two-stroke sports roadster with a similar style to the Paso.

But it was to be the 916 and later still the MV Agusta F4 that were really to cement his design genius.

The designer of the 916, Massimo Tamburini, is one of the truly great men of the late twentieth century motorcycle world.

Based in the principality of San Marino (a tiny province in Italy with its own government and laws) the top-secret Cagiva Research Centre (CRC) is the model, state-of-the-art facility employing the very latest CAD/CAM computer ware.

The 916 project began in the late 1980s and its launch was delayed (as is covered in Chapter 9) by the Cagiva Group's financial problems of the early 1990s. There is no doubt that otherwise this trend-setting design would have been unveiled at least eighteen months to two years earlier.

In Tamburini's own words: 'The theme of the 916 project was to make a sports bike with Italian character, but really different from Japanese bikes ... I wanted to personalize the 916. When you look at it, you know it's a 916 from 200m away; I did this by making the exhaust pipe under the tail. Nobody thought of this before.' He finishes by saying 'the 916 is similar to a wonderful woman. When it goes on to age, it keeps its beauty.'

Tamburini's latest creation is the awe-inspiring MV Agusta F4, which is the only motorcycle on the planet that has challenged the 916 series on visual style.

It is perhaps important for the *Ducatisti* to realize that Massimo Tamburini did not switch to Ducati when Cagiva finally sold their remaining shares to Texas Pacific Group (TPG) in 1998. Pierre Terblanche, who had worked with Tamburini, did switch and is now installed as Ducati chief stylist, in Bologna. This could well prove to be a major problem when Ducati attempt to design the 916's (and of course 748 and 996's) replacement. But of course only time will provide the answer.

Not only did the 916 have style in abundance, but it also had a pedigree that was virtually unmatched in modern motorcycling. Essentially, even in the mass-produced Biposto (twin-seat) form, it was a pure-bred racer, with the bare minimum of equipment necessary to make it street-legal: lights, an electric starter and a number-plate holder! In reality it was nothing less than a production version of similar machines used by the Italian factory to such great effect in the World Super Bike racing championship series (*see* Chapter 8). And remember that Ducati had at that time won all but one of the world titles in the class since the beginning of the 1990s.

MORE POWERFUL ENGINE

Although uprated and with an increase in displacement, the 916's engine unit owed many of its features to the machines it replaced – the 888 and the earlier still 851

An almost completed 916 engine on the factory's production line.

series. All shared the same basic liquid-cooled dohc eight-valve 90-degree V-twin layout, with Weber-Marelli integrated electronic fuel injection and ignition systems.

The 916 (like the 851 and 888) had an engine displacement that matched its model code, achieved by increasing the stroke from 64 to 66mm, the bore remaining unchanged at 94mm. Ducati sources stated maximum power at the crankshaft to be 114bhp at 9,000rpm, with a safe maximum rpm of 10,000. But these figured only gave half the story, the newcomer being much stronger throughout the rev range than the model it replaced. This was thanks to the considerable development time and effort expended by not only Massimo Bordi's engineering team in Bologna, but also by Massimo Tamburini and other members of the Cagiva Research Centre (CRC) based in San Marino. This latter group not only undertook the chassis development, but also the vitally important area of intake and exhaust systems. In fact, much of the 916's development was undertaken by CRC, not Ducati. The reader should be aware of the close co-operation between the Ducati and Cagiva brand names at that time.

SUPERB BUILD

Another vital facet of the 916 project was the use of Cagiva's 500GP-developed RAM (ram-effect – pressurized airbox) air-duct system. This is best described as a force-fed ram-type arrangement similar to that employed on the large Kawasakis, where air is forced into a pressurized sealed container through ducts in the front of the fairing. In addition, the 916 used this airbox as a stressed frame member; on the SP versions this was manufactured in carbon-fibre. As a further point of interest, this actually ensured that the 916 steel trellis frame was stiffer than Cagiva's 500GP bike!

Factory personnel working on a couple of 916 Strada models, circa 1994.

As for the chrome-moly steel frame itself, this was entirely new – even though the basic format could trace its ancestry back to the original 500SL Pantah of the late 1970s. The 916 version benefited compared to the original thanks to the advent of CAD (computer-aided design), which calculated the best balance between outright strength with a high resistance to bending loads and maintaining the lowest possible weight.

The beautiful single-sided swinging arm utilized the latest construction techniques, including the use of hi-tech chilled aluminium alloy and a 'closed differential' section. A stub axle was fastened to the swinging arm via an eccentric hub to allow easy chain adjustment. There was a single large diameter nut for speeding up wheel removal.

The rear suspension (using a Japanese-made Showa single shock), worked through a newly designed linkage system, which increased wheel travel to 130mm and employed steel and Teflon ball joints to ensure prompt and precise response. At the front end of the bike a set of 43mm inverted (upside-down) Showa forks provided an excellent combination of strength and suppleness in this important area.

A feature of the 916 was its patented adjustable steering headset, which allowed the rider to 'tune in' the steering geometry of his choice to suit track conditions or personal preferences. Except for specialist, limited-built, hyper-expensive machines such as Bimota, Ducati became the first mainstream motorcycle manufacturer to offer such a feature in its standard production models. The rake/trail settings available were 24 degrees of rake with 94mm of trail, or 25 degrees of rake with 100mm of trail.

Another guide to the design team's attention to detail were the wheels. The front component, with a 3.5in rim, used a unique angled valve stem. This may seem a small point, but it was a significant feature, allowing as it did easy access for a tyre pressure gauge. The 5.5in rear rim was also of a special design, enabling it to function with the sexy single-sided swinging arm.

Due to intricate tuning and balancing of the radical stainless steel exhaust pipes and updating of the fuel injection monitoring and

The 916 Strada (1994)

Engine	Liquid-cooled, dohc, 4-valves-per-cylinder, 90-degree V-twin, belt-driven overhead camshafts
Bore and stroke	94 × 66mm
Displacement	916cc
Compression ratio	11.2:1
Maximum power (at crank)	109bhp @ 9,000rpm
Lubrication	Forced feed gear pump, with oil cooler
Ignition	Electronic IAW type
Fuel system	Weber-Marelli electronic indirect type
Primary drive	Straight cut gears (crank 31 teeth, clutch 62 teeth)
Final drive	Chain 525HV (gearbox sprocket 15 teeth, rear wheel 36 teeth)
Gearbox	6 speeds, straight cut gears
Frame	Lattice type, round steel ALS 450
Front suspension	Inverted telescopic fork with 43mm stanchion diameter, fully adjustable. Travel 127mm
Rear suspension	Progressive linkage with adjustable monoshock. Shock travel 71mm, wheel travel 130mm
Front brake	Twin 320mm Brembo brake discs, 4-piston calipers
Rear brake	Single 220mm disc, 2-piston calliper
Wheels	3-spoke, light alloy
Front tyre	120/70 17in
Rear tyre	190/50 17in

This and following detail shots of a 1994 916 Strada (the first of the 916 series to enter production) attempt to show the main features of interest in this trend-setting design. This fairing-off shot illustrates how compactly everything is laid out under the bodywork.

The 916 Strada (1994) (*continued*)

Nearside view of 916 engine and its ancillary equipment, such as radiator, oil cooler, injectors / airbox, sensors and external engine piping.

(Left) *This overhead view shows not just another angle of the injectors / airbox, but also many other features, such as top frame rail layout, cross-mounted hydraulic steering damper, adjustable steering head-set, instrumentation, clutch and front brake master cylinders, and the rider's controls and switchgear.*

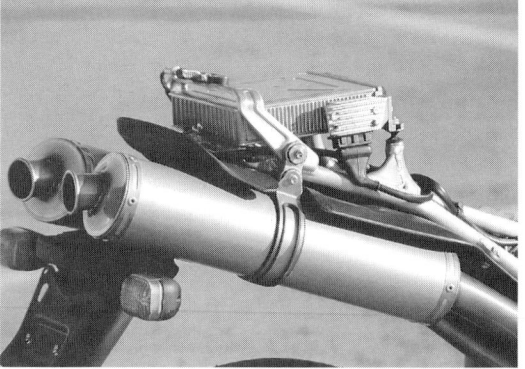

(Above) *Note the neat installation of the machine's computer 'brain' and end cans (mufflers). There is not a single piece of wasted space here.*

The original 1994 916 Strada with its single seat. Note the seat vents and dual rear lights.

Valve sizes	Inlet 33mm, exhaust 29mm
Valve timing	Inlet opens 11 BTDC/ closes 70 ABCD Exhaust opens 62 BBDC/ closes 18 ATDC
Length	80in (2,030mm)
Width	30.7in (780mm)
Height	42.5in (1,080mm)
Seat height	31in (790mm)
Ground clearance	6in (150mm)
Fuel tank capacity	17 litres (3.75imp. gal)
Dry weight	450lb (204kg)
Maximum speed	161.5mph (260km/h)

Single-side swinging arm, three-spoke alloy wheels and hi-level exhaust – all features of the 916 Strada.

metering systems, the factory was able to claim that the larger displacement, longer-stroke motor provided increased power and torque throughout the entire rev range.

Besides the longer stroke and its resultant capacity increase, other significant engine improvements had been made, notably to the crankcases (a definite weakness on the 888 engine, particularly under racing conditions) and of the valve material itself. This latter improvement had a visible benefit to owners in the form of longer service intervals between valve adjustments.

Of all the 916's styling features the three that really grabbed attention, however, were the single-sided swinging arm, the exhaust system which exited through a pair of silencers just underneath the seat, and the ultra-distinctive bodywork, particularly the twin 'pillar-box' headlamps for their curvaceous fairing.

PRESS REACTION

Ducati's PR department had an easy job of getting press coverage: the bike itself said everything. Journalists all around the world were falling over themselves to heap praise on the newcomer. Alan Cathcart, writing in *Cycle Canada*, was typical when he said: 'A bike whose excellence is immediately apparent with no rough edges to be addressed; it abounds with evidence of care and thought, from major aspects like suspension and steering to a host of minor details that compose this piece of mechanical art.' Cathcart went on to add, 'the finest street bike I have ever ridden, from any manufacturer, in any country'.

One of the 916's greatest assets was its ability to transfer all its available power onto the tarmac, the throttle response being out of the top drawer. *Motor Cycle News* highlighted this asset in a May 1994 test, in which the

Ducati went head-to-head with Honda's best selling CBR 900RR Fireblade, saying: 'It [the 916] has the best fuel injection available on a production bike, no question. There's none of the on-off delivery of the RC45, and the carburation is clean and ultra-responsive from tickover to the red line. Whatever the track times say, the Ducati feels quicker than the Honda, and feels better doing it.'

Other typical 1994-launch time quotes from the pressmen included: 'An ace move which has made the 916 something not even fully paid-up self-confessed junkies of the 888SP possibly thought it could be – the best road bike in the world' (*Fast Bikes*), and 'It's the best finished motorcycle ever to come out of Italy!' (*Superbike*). Even two years later, in March 1996, *MCN* were still just as enthusiastic:

> Ducati's 916 has the best track record of any current bike, dominating the world and British superbike championships. And like the racer, the production machine uses the principle of excellent all-round balance rather than outright power to keep up with its Japanese four-cylinder rivals. A deficiency in power and more weight than the Honda (Fireblade) and Suzuki (GSX-R750WT), are overcome by making more effective use of the engine and chassis.

In a giant test in the June 1996 issue of *Bike* the tester said: 'The 916 oozes charm and attracts attention wherever it goes. Its sculpted lines and sleek looks make it an instant classic, which is more than can be said of any of the others.' 'The others' in this case were Kawasaki's ZX-7R, Suzuki's GSX-R750, Honda's Fireblade and Yamaha's YZF 1000 Thunderace. *Bike* electronically timed the 916 (Biposto) at 161.4mph (259.7km/h), with the standing start quarter mile being polished off in 11.20 seconds – with a terminal speed of 126.1mph (202.9km/h).

Cagiva Mito Evo – a miniature 916

If you cannot afford a 916 (or a 748/996) and want the looks, there's only one answer – the Cagiva Mito Evo (Evolution).

Launched onto the market at the same time as the 916 (spring 1994) the Mito Evo was styled by the same man as its bigger Ducati cousin, Massimo Tamburini. Both come from the CRC (Cagiva Research Centre). Tamburini's CV is impressive: co-founder of Bimota in the early 1970s, he joined Cagiva in the mid 1980s, with the Ducati Paso – his first styling exercise for his new employers – making its debut at the 1985 Milan Show. But the 916 was his big triumph. No wonder the then Ducati owners, Cagiva, 'borrowed' the same sexy style.

Together with the Aprilia RS125 Extrema, the Cagiva Mito Evo has been good enough to have lead the world of sports 125 street bikes for half a decade since its 1994 launch and still seems fresh today. To be honest, from the front it is difficult to tell the 916 and the Cagiva apart; that is, until the engine is started and instead of a booming V-twin four-stroke, all you get is a smoky single-pot two-stroke.

However, as *Motor Cycle News* said in their 17 May 1995 group test: 'For sheer excitement no bikes can match the excitement of the new breed of lightweight 125s. Outbraking and outcornering virtually all other road bikes, the latest range of unrestricted 125s offer serious fun – and 100mph performance!'

And of the four bikes tested (the others were the Aprilia, Yamaha TZR and Suzuki RGV) the Cagiva was the quickest through the MCN electronic speed trap, clocking 102.1mph (164.3km/h).

Then there was the limited production Mito Evo SP (Sport Production), which, as delivered from the factory, produced 32bhp and could top 110mph (177km/h) in road-going trim.

I had the job of running the official Cagiva (backed by importers Three Cross) team in the British SuperTeen racing series during 1995 and 1996, winning the 1995 title along the way, so can report that a blueprinted Mito Evo is good for 36bhp and 125mph in racing mode – some performance for what is after all a single-cylinder engine of only 124.6cc (56×50.5mm) with reed valve induction, exhaust valves and 35mm carburettor.

But I'll let *Motor Cycle News* have the final say from their May 1995 test: 'Sexy Mito mimics the gorgeous looks of much lusted after Ducati 916, no wonder it draws so much attention from onlookers.'

From many angles the Cagiva Mito Evo (introduced the same year as the 916 – 1994) can be mistaken for one of the Ducati V-twins; that is until the engine is started! Another styling masterpiece by Massimo Tamburini.

916 VARIANTS AND MODIFICATIONS

The 916 was built in the following guises (discounting of course pure racing versions, which in any case had different engine capacities and are described elsewhere):

916 Strada (single seat)	1994–96
916 SP	1995
916 Biposto (dual seat)	1995–98
916 SPS	1997–98
916 Senna I	1995
916 Senna II	1997
916 Senna III	1998

The 916 SP (Sport Production) differed from the 916 BP (Biposto) in having increased power, carbon-fibre fairing and silencers, an Öhlins rear shock, cast iron fully floating

---

The 916 SP (1995)

Engine	Liquid-cooled, dohc, 4-valves-per-cylinder, 90-degree V-twin, belt-driven overhead camshafts
Bore and stroke	94 × 66mm
Displacement	916cc
Compression ratio	11.2:1
Maximum power (at crank)	131bhp @ 10,500rpm
Lubrication	Forced feed gear pump, with oil cooler
Ignition	Electronic IAW type
Fuel system	Weber-Marelli electronic indirect type
Primary drive	Straight cut gears (crank 31 teeth, clutch 62 teeth)
Final drive	Chain 525 HV (gearbox sprocket 14 teeth, rear wheel 36 teeth)
Gearbox	6 speeds, straight cut gears
Frame	Lattice type, round steel ALS 450
Front suspension	Inverted telescopic fork with 43mm stanchion diameter, fully adjustable. Travel 120mm
Rear suspension	Progressive linkage with adjustable monoshock, shock travel 71mm, wheel travel 130mm
Front brake	Twin 320mm Brembo brake discs, 4-piston calipers
Rear brake	Single 220mm disc, 2-piston calliper
Wheels	3-spoke, light alloy
Front tyre	120/70 17in
Rear tyre	190/50 17in
Valve sizes	Inlet 34mm, exhaust 30mm
Valve timing	Inlet opens 53 BTDC/closes 71 ABDC
	Exhaust opens 77 BBDC/closes 42 ATDC
Length	80.7in (2,050mm)
Width	27in (685mm)
Height	43in (1,090mm)
Seat height	31in (790mm)
Ground clearance	6in (150mm)
Fuel tank capacity	17 litres (3.75imp. gal)
Dry weight	430lb (195kg)
Maximum speed	168mph (270km/h)

*Many owners like to customize their own particular bike. Roy Fuller's 1995 916 BP is a good example –
Aeroquip braided brake lines, EBC racing brake pods and Pro-lite composite racing discs; Marchesini
wheels; Pirelli Corsa tyres; big-bore exhaust with F1 carbon-fibre cans; carbon-fibre heel guides and
exhaust pipe heat shields. Even the computer chip has been remapped by Devimead Racing.*

*Status symbol that it is, the 916
often appears in many forms of
advertising. This colourful
postcard promoting an Italian
restaurant is typical.*

Ayrton Senna

Before his tragic and untimely death at Imola in the summer of 1994, Ayrton Senna had visited the Ducati factory in Bologna to approve a motorcycle that was to bear his name, the 916 Senna, on 7 March that year.

In the two years prior to his death Senna had dedicated himself to the foundation bearing his name. Amongst its objectives was the development and implementation of health and support programmes for children and young people from all over the world. To achieve the necessary funding a commercial company, Ayrton Senna Licensing, was set up to underpin the project.

The Castiglioni brothers Gianfranco and Claudio (co-owners of Ducati at that time) had close links with the F1 car scene so it was perhaps to be expected that a personal – and business – friendship should develop between them and Senna. The visible proof of this was the Ducati Senna project.

Essentially a special limited edition 916, these machines are likely (as with the Fogarty replica – *see* Chapter 12) to become collector's pieces as time goes on – in much the same way as the limited edition round-case Imola replica 750 SS bevel V-twin of the mid-1970s has.

The late Ayrton Senna, one of the great motor racing drivers of the late twentieth century.

The Senna Licensing company donates all profits from licensing contracts to the Ayrton Senna Foundation, and is overseen by Ayrton's sister.

The first batch of machines (Senna I), totalling 300 units, came off the Bologna production line in 1995, and approximately the same number of Senna IIs were built and sold in 1997. The final mark was the series III. Built in 1998, these were the last ones, as this is what the original agreement allowed for. My understanding is that no more than 1,000 Sennas of all marks were built.

The Senna I was finished in dark metallic grey with brick red wheels, gold handlebar lever supports and a silver plaque with a progressive production number (on the top fork yoke), a special motorcycle cloth cover and a certification document.

Ayrton Senna (left) and Ducati boss Claudio Castiglioni (right) meeting in March 1994.

In the tech-spec department all Sennas largely followed the standard 916 BP rather than the SP/SPS versions, but with the following changes: single seat, carbon-fibre chainguard, front mudguard and clutch cover, aluminium rear subframe, alternative racing EPROM for the fuel injection system, Öhlins rear shock; cast iron fully floating discs and braided hoses for the front brakes, adjustable brake and clutch levers. The Senna II was essentially unchanged except for a move to light metallic grey for the body parts (carbon-fibre items excluded).

All Sennas were supplied 'street ready', as the factory called it. This meant they came with road-legal aluminium silencers – carbon-fibre 'cans' being supplied separately and inscribed 'for race use only'.

The Senna I, which arrived in 1995, instantly became a collectable classic, even though it owed more to the standard 916 BP than the racier SP version.

Next came the Senna II for the 1997 model year. No Sennas were built in 1996 because of the company's financial problems at the time.

The final batch of 300 Sennas (the III) arrived in 1998. A total of 900 examples of all Sennas were constructed. The original agreement did not allow for any more than this.

A dual seat BP (Biposto) version of the 916 arrived in 1996. But although there are pillion footrests, the riding pillion is not a particularly comfortable experience – although many passengers put up with it for the sight and sound of this truly sexy motorcycle.

front brake discs, braided front brake hoses, adjustable brake and clutch levers and, of course, a single seat.

For the 1997 model year the 916 SPS arrived. This was conceived so the bike could be homologated for SBK/FIM Sport Production racing events.

Based on the 916 SP, the SPS had the larger WSB-derived 996cc (98 × 66mm) engine size, cast iron fully floating brake discs, braided front brake, clutch and rear brake metal pipes, a front headlamp with dual parking light and wiring, modified final drive ratio, silver plate on top of steering yoke for individual series number, improved half handlebar fixing, performance muffler kit and performance computer chip.

For 1998 the 916 series remained largely unchanged except that at last it became available (in BP form) in the yellow that was so popular in the 748 series. Later in the year the limited edition Fogarty Replica version of the 996cc SPS made its debut on the UK market.

But after five years the factory decided to axe the 916 model code for the 1999 model year in favour of the 996. And, as is revealed in Chapter 11, no more machines would be built with 916cc; from now on all would be

996 – as had been the case with the racing machines for some time.

A fitting tribute is an extract from a British test of the model which says it all:

The 916 shape is distinctive and is likely to be remembered and revered as long as Jaguar's E-type car.

(*Motor Cycle News*).

(Above) *The all-singing and all-dancing 916 SPS was introduced for the 1997 model year. This was in fact a 996cc (98 × 66mm), and the first use of this larger engine size for street use. Made with lightweight material, the weight dropped from 450lb (204kg) for the BP model down to a low 419lb (190kg) for the more exotic SPS. This, and the increase in power output and torque, gave blistering performance.*

Another area that has proved popular for the 916 is track days. As the model is so closely linked to the circuit through its racing brothers, many owners like to try their hand without actually entering a race. Track days are an obvious substitute. This rider is Jeffrey Collins, seen on his 916 SP at Brands Hatch in March 1998.

Pro Twins

Pro Twins are the guys who were behind a tasty conversion of what had been a standard 1998 916 SPS (996!) purchased from London dealers Frontiers by owner Kelvin Russell (a leading London banking executive).

Based in South Godstone, Surrey, Pro Twins was formed in late 1997 by three partners from very different backgrounds, each bringing their own individual skill to the organization. The first is former racer aeronautical engineer Robert Jackson, who was born and bred in Brisbane, Australia. Next in the trio is Peter Ramsey, a mechanic for all his working life, the last four years working solely with Ducatis. In the winter of 1997–98 he spannered for the American Fast by Ferracci squad, helping prepare engines for Daytona. Third, but not least, is Brett Norris, the 'businessman', a former telecommunications specialist by trade – and, like the others, a fanatical bike enthusiast.

Kelvin Russell's first contact with Pro Twins came at a Moto Cinelli track day, where he was given assistance by Rob Jackson, who was attending the event. This led to Kelvin paying Pro Twins a number of visits. Wanting a machine that would have a unique identity he entrusted his SPS to the South Godstone-based concern. The result was a faster, lighter, quickly steering device that could easily be converted from track to road guise.

The engine, with the exception of the gearbox (road ratios) and the need to retain the starter motor, was modified up to 996cc Corsa specification. Lightening was relatively easy, although limited by the need for continued road usage. Carbon-fibre was extensively employed throughout, including a bespoke carbon dash assembly based around the 1995–96 955 Corsa design. Speed and odometer figures were provided digitally via an LCD display in the centre of the analogue tachometer.

In the handling department the machine's geometry was extensively altered through the use of new magnesium fork yokes (triple clamps), a beautifully sculpted magnesium swinging arm and Marchesini wheels. The yokes were modified to provide more trail at the front bringing the engine almost 2mm nearer to the front wheel spindle, whilst the revised swinging arm configuration was engineered 40mm longer making the overall wheel base 20mm longer. Both front and rear suspension springs were changed to progressive units from Dutch specialist, Hyperpro, to aid comfort and help handling on typical less-than-perfect UK road surfaces; both fork sliders were titanium nitrided. The braking components were largely stock, apart from the top-of-the-line Brembo GP 19 × 20mm master cylinder, as favoured by leading racers.

One man's ultimate machine; the Pro Twins 916 SPS owned by London Banker, Kelvin Russell.

7 The 748

The huge success of the 916 led to the launch of the smaller displacement 748, which first went on sale in the spring of 1995. The launch was also a way of gaining yet more success on the race circuit, not in Super Bike competition, but in Super Sport – the European Super Sport championship in fact, which at many meetings was a support to the World Super Bike series itself.

On the road the 748 was very much its own motorcycle, not simply a smaller-engined, cheaper 916. The 748 had its own distinctive character – revvier and smoother power delivery whilst retaining its bigger brother's handling, braking and looks. In fact many owners swear the 748 is a better choice for them than the 916 (or for that matter, its successor, the 996).

At first there were only two versions of the 748, the Biposto (dual seat) and SP (Sport Production). The latter differed from the Biposto in having increased power, carbon-

The 748 arrived in spring 1995, a year after its bigger brother, the 916. It was offered in both SP (seen here) and BP versions that year.

fibre fairing and silencers, an Öhlins rear shock, cast iron fully floating front brake discs, metal braided front brake lines, adjustable brake and clutch levers and, of course, a single seat.

When first deliveries of the 748 SP arrived in April 1995 it soon found its way onto the race circuit both in official factory entries and the privateers. In Britain, unlike the rest of Europe, politics conspired to restrict the 748's competition career to 1995 only. And it must be said that even then it was a particularly unhappy affair. Only four riders were actually entered on the Bologna Vs in what was billed as the British Supercup 1995 Super Sport 600. The four were Jason Emmett (brother of Sean), who rode for *Fast Bikes* magazine, Pete Jennings, Ivan Carter and New Zealander Robert Holden. None of these four completed the season: Emmett

The 748 Biposto (1995)

Engine	Liquid-cooled, dohc, 4-valves-per-cylinder, 90-degree V-twin, belt-driven overhead camshafts
Bore and stroke	88 × 61.5mm
Displacement	748cc
Compression ratio	11.5:1
Maximum power (at crank)	97bhp @ 11,000rpm
Lubrication	Forced feed gear pump, with oil cooler
Ignition	Electronic IAW type
Fuel system	Weber-Marelli electronic indirect type, one injector per cylinder
Primary drive	Straight cut gears (crank 31 teeth, clutch 62 teeth)
Final drive	Chain DID 520 VL4 (gearbox sprocket 14 teeth, rear wheel 38 teeth)
Gearbox	6 speeds, straight cut gears
Frame	Lattice type, round steel ALS 450
Front suspension	Inverted telescopic fork with 43mm stanchion diameter, fully adjustable. Travel 127mm
Rear suspension	Progressive linkage with adjustable monoshock. Shock travel 71mm, wheel travel 130mm
Front brake	Twin 320mm Brembo brake discs, 4-piston calipers
Rear brake	Single 245mm (220mm 1996 onwards) disc, 20-piston caliper
Wheels	3-spoke, light alloy
Front tyre	120/70 17in
Rear tyre	180/55 17in
Valve sizes	Inlet 33mm, exhaust 29mm
Valve timing	Inlet opens 11 BTDC/closes 70 ABDC
	Exhaust opens 62 BBDC/closes 18 ATDC
Length	80in (2,030mm)
Width	30.7in (780mm)
Height	42.5in (1,080mm)
Seat height	31in (790mm)
Ground clearance	6in (150mm)
Fuel tank capacity	17 litres (3.75imp. gal)
Dry weight	445lb (202kg)
Maximum speed	152mph (245km/h)

Unlike the 916, the 748 was offered from its first days in a choice of both red (as here) and yellow.

and Jennings struck a series of mechanical disasters; Holden suffered a fatal accident whilst riding one of the larger Ducati V-twins on a Sports Motorcycles-entered machine in the Isle of Man TT; and former SuperTeen racer Carter (who bought an entirely stock, straight out-of-the-crate 748SP from his local dealer Thruxton Motorcycles of Andover, Hampshire) was forced out after only a few rounds due to financial pressures. Pete Jennings posed a serious challenge to the rest of the competition while his bike was going, and for the first third of the season (up to June) led the championships, before being forced to switch to a Honda CBR600.

It is also worth noting that whilst the basic 748 engine used 916 components,

there were some cost savings. For example, the expensive Austrian Pankl connecting rods found on the higher performance versions of the 916 series were not used. Instead, during 1995 the 748SP used an H-section steel type. Furthermore, from the 1998 model year onwards titanium rods have been used, even though the 'official' line is that 'there were no problems'.

For the 1997 model year the 748 range was widened to include the 748 S – also known as the Monoposto (single seat). This model fitted between the BP (Biposto) and SP models, being essentially a BP, but with a single saddle, aluminium rear sub-frame, Öhlins shock, cast iron front discs, braided metal front brake pipes, together with a standard issue motorcycle cover and paddock stand.

A 748 SP (Sport Production) under test in the summer of 1995.

When the 1998 model range was announced there were three 748s: the Hyper Sport (formerly Biposto); Hyper Sport SPS and the racing only 748R; the latter was intended for European Super Sport competition.

Due to its continued success the 748 has received very few changes to its specification, but for the 1999 model year updates were made, but in detail rather than major

1998 748 Models Dry Weight Figures	
Hyper Sport 748	432lb (196kg)
Hyper Sport 748 SPS	428lb (194kg)
Racing 748 R	375lb (170kg)

An owner's view

It's that time of year again – the Bike show – so I'm on the M6 heading for the NEC (Birmingham) and I'm thinking to myself, 'What would I replace the 748 with?'

I grew up with British Twins, so becoming a 'born again biker' subsequently owning and riding modern multi-cylinder superbikes proved to be a revelation: no more twins for me, or so I thought. Then, and as the Italians say, *'mama mia'*, there it was – slim, sensuous, desirable and red. 'The Duke.' I had to have it.

Everything ever said about this magnificent machine is true. Bucket loads of Italian style abound, that magical, rhythmic growl from the exhaust, more especially evident from a pair of Termagonis and that precise handling aided by the wonderfully torquey twin-cylinder jewel of an engine. Standing still or in action, this is a glorious picture.

My first impressions of the Duke is how small it seems, how narrow and slender in profile. With the aggressive riding position, moving body weight over the front wheel, if you open the throttle and close your eyes (for a second!), it could be Monza and the Tiffosi or even Carl's team-mate … Dream on!

On the move the racing pedigree becomes very apparent, with sharp handling, endless pulling power (in every sense of the word) and that seductive, if slightly illegal, exhaust note.

So is there a down side? Well, sadly, yes there is: the overall poor condition of our British roads, especially in the south-east, make absolute enjoyment a bit difficult. Any good tarmac surface, such as a race track, provides the Duke's rider the maximum opportunity to enjoy the excellent temperament this machine affords.

So, the show is over, I'm on my way home, it was a great day out and I'm reflecting on my original thoughts 'What would I replace the Duke with? Dead easy … another!'

Doug Flory, 49, Ipswich, Suffolk; owner of a 748 Biposto

The 748 is, if anything, a better all-round package than the 916. Certainly the grin factor, as the author's friend George Paget is demonstrating here, is huge.

(Below) *A line-up of 748 BPs await crating at the factory, December 1997.*

1998 Ducati 748 Biposto road test by Rod Woolnough

The most fun I've ever had on a motorbike. Riding the 748 Biposto was a revelation. Despite having spent much of the last 30 years riding sports motorcycles as fast as possible, I had no idea that the kind of performance provided by this Ducati was available to the road rider. It has re-written the rulebook as far as I am concerned.

The 748 is an absolutely gorgeous bike. The one I tested, a 1998 Biposto, was painted in yellow. I wouldn't have one in any other colour. It is a tiny bike and I am sure that the yellow paint creates the illusion that it is even smaller than it really is. Most of its component parts are shared with its big brother, the 916, but the 748 felt so much smaller.

I took the 748 to the Isle of Man for the 1998 Manx Grand Prix races, my wife, Liz, perched on the back. The 350-mile ride up to Heysham from Stamford, Lincolnshire passed in a flash. When we reached the ferry terminal we were disappointed to have arrived so quickly. We could have ridden for many more hours in perfect comfort and we were having so much fun! I'm 6ft tall and generously proportioned, but the seat, footrest, handlebar relationship suited me perfectly, and the sculpted tank could have been made specifically for me, my arms and legs fitted into it so neatly. Liz was in an equally comfortable position on the back. Her 5ft 2in, 7-stone frame found itself perfectly suited to life as a pillion passenger on the 748.

The 'little' Ducati doesn't have a lot of power at low revs but is quite happy to trundle around town. On the open roads, given full throttle at 5,000rpm or more and the 748 starts to pull hard. At 7,000 revs the induction roar hardens to a rising howl, 8,000 and it's off, 9, 10, 11, 12,000, it's intoxicating, up a gear, right into the power again. In 6th gear it's doing 150mph, two up and it's thrilling. The bike is impossibly nimble. It steers quickly and flicks from one side to the other so easily, with angles of lean that I'd previously only dreamt of, but always feeling completely secure. We knew, corner after corner, that, although we had never been round those bends quite so quickly before, that we could have gone even faster. Off the TT circuit the island's roads are much bumpier. Initially cautious, we soon found that, although the suspension on this particular bike was set up really hard and very damped, we could ride as quickly as we liked. The most amazing revelation was that the 748 would still hold a perfect line on corner exits even when the rising power and bumpy surface conspired to throw the front wheel high into the air with the bike cranked hard over. I've never known anything like it. Sometimes we even had it leant over, both wheels off the ground and it still kept its line. The hard suspension did, however, ensure that at speed over these bumpy back roads both rider and passenger, particularly Liz, spent a lot of time getting their bottoms smacked by their respective seats! We didn't mind at all!

This 748 BP has the giant Laxey Wheel as its backdrop during an extended test by Rod Woolnough, September 1998.

The Isle of Man again. A quarter of a century separates the 1973 Sport bevel V-twin in the background and Woolnough's importer-supplied test 748 BP. Besides the yellow colour schemes both old and new Ducati V-twins also shared the 748cc displacement.

The controls were perfectly positioned, with adjustable hand levers and beautifully crafted foot pedals. The sidestand always worried us, but the bike didn't fall over! There were no complaints about the switchgear. The lights were very good, perfectly suited for riding at high speed during the hours of darkness. The mirrors were good, never folding back at speed and only needing a slight tuck of the elbow and tiny head movement to give a wide view of the road behind. The clutch action and gearchange were light and exceptionally slick. The back brake, however, didn't really do anything except make a nasty, brake pad on fire, type of smell! Who needs a back brake! Actually, it did work at low speeds, where it helped with bike control. The front brake was as powerful and progressive as you could wish. It became usual to steam into corners still braking hard as the bike leant over further and further, let go of the brake, lay it right down, pick it up again and wheelie out with a twist of the throttle. The 748 made this sort of riding easy. It felt natural. It's the very best way to travel.

The yellow test bike attracted a lot of attention and it deserved it. It really is a pretty motorcycle. We spent a lot of time just revelling in its beauty; we just couldn't leave it alone. Either riding it or looking at it, my wife and I loved it. We parked it at Hawthorne Inn, on the TT course, next to the landlord's 70s 750S, the lovely yellow one. The landlord, Paul Summerfield, his wife, Verley, and their baby son, Tom, were ecstatic. The two bikes together were a special sight. Both had an engine capacity of 748cc. The 1998 748 made a worthy successor to that early twin, we all agreed to that.

Eventually, the Manx Grand Prix was over for another year and we had to return to the mainland and give the bike back to Moto Cinelli, the UK Ducati importers who had kindly provided the test bike. We found it very difficult to part with and to this day regret not having bought the 748 from them there and then. We had travelled 2,250 miles in three weeks, mostly at high speed on the Isle of Man and had no mishaps, no frightening moments, just the most fun we'd ever had on a motorcycle.

alterations. The 1999 748 Biposto was given SPS-style front brakes – in other words discs in 4mm steel – new flange fitment, wider type calipers, a PSC16 master cylinder and metal braided brake pipes. The rear brake system was also updated to SPS specification. The front fork sliders featured a modified lug to fit wider calipers. A new PSC13 clutch master cylinder was fitted, together with a braided metal clutch line pre-assembled with piston.

The handlebar braces now featured two screws. And finally, the graphics for the fairing and tank were updated, the word 'Ducati' making a reappearance on the fuel tank sides by popular demand.

The only changes on the 748 SPS were to make the silencers slightly bigger and update the fairing and tank graphics in a similar fashion to the Biposto. After all, why change a winning formula just for the sake of it?

The 748 SPS (1999)

Engine	Liquid-cooled, dohc, 4-valves-per-cylinder, 90-degree V-twins, belt-driven overhead camshafts
Bore and stroke	88×61.5mm
Displacement	748cc
Compression ratio	11.6:1
Maximum power (at crank)	104bhp @ 11,000rpm
Lubrication	Forced feed gear pump, with oil cooler
Ignition	Electronic IAW type
Fuel system	Weber-Marelli electronic indirect type CPU 1.6
Primary drive	Straight cut gears (crank 31 teeth; clutch 62 teeth)
Final drive	Chain DID 520 VL4 (gearbox sprocket 14 teeth; rear wheel 37 teeth)
Gearbox	6 speeds, straight cut gears
Frame	Lattice type, round steel 25 chrome molybdenum$_4$
Front suspension	Inverted telescopic fork with 43mm stanchion diameter, fully adjustable. Travel 127mm
Rear suspension	Progressive linkage with adjustable monoshock. Shock travel 71mm, wheel travel 130mm
Front brake	Twin 320mm fully floating Brembo brake discs, 4-piston calipers
Rear brake	Single 220mm disc 2-piston calliper
Wheels	3-spoke light alloy
Front tyre	120/60 ZR 17in
Rear tyre	180/55 ZR 17in
Valve sizes	Inlet 33mm, exhaust 29mm
Valve timing	Inlet opens 44 BTDC/closes 72 ABDC
	Exhaust opens 77 BBDC/closes 42 ATDC
Length	80in (2,030mm)
Width	30.7in (780mm)
Height	42.5in (1,080mm)
Seat height	31in (790mm)
Ground clearance	6in (150mm)
Fuel tank capacity	17 litres (3.75imp. gal)
Dry weight	428lb (194kg)
Maximum speed	155mph (250km/h)

World Super Sport Championship

The Super Sport category, created in 1990, reached its peak in 1996, the year in which all the rounds of the championship were run at the same events as World Super Bike.

This category, similar in concept to World Super Bike, represents a challenge for the manufacturers, who are required to comply with very tight rule restrictions. Exclusively four-stroke machines are allowed to take part in the championship: 600cc four-cylinder bikes and 750cc twin-cylinder bikes, with a minimum weight for all machines of 172kg (378lb). The technical level therefore presents very few differences from the production model available for the general public. This gives enormous advantage in terms of running costs and balanced racing.

In 1999 the eleven events on the Super Sport calendar are due to be held together with the World Super Bike races.

Besides their World Super Bike successes, Ducati have also been extremely active in the Super Sport series. For either 600cc four-cylinders or 750cc twins, the Super Sport World Championships have run alongside WSB since 1996. The first champion was Fabrizio Pirovano, seen here that year on his 748.

World Super Sport Championship Calendar: Eleven Rounds

28 Mar	Kyalami	South Africa
2 May	Donington	Great Britain
16 May	Albacete	Spain
30 May	Monza	Italy
13 Jun	Nurburgring	Germany
27 Jun	Misano Adriatico	San Marino
11 Jul	Laguna Seca	USA
1 Aug	Brands Hatch	Europe
29 Aug	A1-Ring	Austria
5 Sep	Assen	Netherlands
12 Sep	Hockenheim	Germany

Super Sports Championship Winners

1996	Fabrizio Pirovano	Ducati
1997	Paolo Casoli	Ducati
1998	Fabrizio Pirovano	Suzuki

Team Ducati Performance – 1999 World Super Sport Championship

Team Manager
Davide Tardozzi

Rider
Paolo Casoli

Chief Engineer, Ducati Corse
Corrado Cecchinelli

Paolo Casoli's Technical Crew

Domenico Brigaglia	Team manager and chief mechanic
Denis Pani	Electronics engineer
Davide Manfredi	Mechanic

Claudio Montanari	Mechanic
Pietro Massari	Mechanic

Technical Components Engineer
Maurizio Perlini

Press Officer
Michele Morisetti, Ducati Corse

Hospitality and PR
Paola Braiato, Ducati Corse

Photographer
Fabrizio Porrozzi

Paolo Casoli

The talented Paolo Casoli, 1997 Super Sport World Champion on a Ducati 748, will in 1999 be involved on two fronts: Ducati Performance rider in the World Super Sport Championship and official Ducati Corse test-rider in the Italian Super Bike Championship. The five events in the Italian championship are an excellent testbed for the 996 Superbike 'evolution' projects.

Paolo Casoli was born on 18 August 1965 at Castelnuovo ne' Monti (Reggio Emilia province). He is married to Catia and they have one son, Federico. His first race was the 1982 FMI Junior TT-F4 Trophy at Vallelunga on a Villa 125.

Career

Year	Position	Competition	Team
1982	5th	FMI Junior TT-F4 Trophy	Villa
1983	2nd	Italian Junior 125 Championship	MBA
1984	8th	European 125 Championship	MBA
1985	3rd	European 125 Championship	MBA
1986	14th	World 125 Championship	MBA
1987	3rd	World 125 Championship	MBA
1988	44th	World 250 Championship	Garelli
1989	35th	World 250 Championship	Honda
1990	16th	World 250 Championship	Yamaha
1991	10th	World 250 Championship	Yamaha
1992	17th	World 250 Championship	Yamaha
1993	23rd	World 250 Championship	Gilera
1994	13th	World Super Bike Championship	Yamaha
1995	1st	Italian Super Bike Championship	Yamaha
	16th	World Super Bike Championship	Yamaha
1996	1st	Italian Super Bike Championship	(Ducati Gio.Ca.Moto)
	14th	World Super Bike Championship	(Ducati Gio.Ca.Moto)
1997	1st	World Super Sport Championship	(Ducati Gio.Ca.Moto)
	1st	Italian Super Sport Championship	(Ducati Gio.Ca.Moto)
1998	4th	World Super Sport Championship	(Ducati Performance)

Ducati 748

Engine	Liquid-cooled, 90° V-twin four stroke
Bore and stroke	88 × 61.5mm
Displacement	748cc
Brake horsepower	112bhp @ 11,500rpm
Ignition	Magneti Marelli
Fuel system	Electronic injection
Frame	Steel trestle
Front suspension	Upside-down fork
Rear suspension	Öhlins single shock absorber
Front brake	Twin 320mm Brembo disk brakes, Brembo 4-piston calipers
Rear brake	Brembo 2-piston caliper
Tyres	Michelin

8 The V-Twins on the Race Track

At the beginning of the 1980s Ducati garnered no fewer than four racing world championship titles – in 1981–84 – thanks to Englishman Tony Rutter's feats aboard a succession of Pantah-based TT Formula V-twins. Rutter could well have won yet another title in 1985 but for a serious accident sustained whilst racing at Montjuic Park, Barcelona, that year.

Back in 1983 another four-times world champion (all gained on Harley-Davidson two-strokes in the mid-1970s), Walter Villa, had ridden a new 748.1cc (88×61.5mm) version of the TTF2 belt-driven Pantah engine, officially coded TTF1. In order to construct this particular powerplant changes were required to the crankcases. Unlike the earlier form of monoshock suspension used on the TTF2, the F1's rear suspension was of the more modern (and efficient) rising rate variety.

It should be remembered that the building of this (and Rutter's bikes) came at a time of great turmoil for the factory. In fact it would be true to say it was a miracle that Ducati went racing at all. The bike's development was also badly affected by the political events that were happening at the very time of its debut in the spring of 1983 (see Chapters 1 and 9). Finally, on 1 May 1985, the Castiglioni brothers gained control of Ducati, and their Cagiva organization set about making up for lost time – both on the production front and the race circuit.

Almost instantly, it seemed, came news of fresh developments, both street and track, at breakneck speed, such was the new owners' enthusiasm for the task they had set themselves of rebuilding Ducati as a world force.

This period coincided with Massimo Bordi taking over the reins of chief designer in place of the legendary, but by now elderly, Ing. Fabio Taglioni, who was in the process of retiring. Taglioni did not simply retire from his job in one move; instead his retirement was spread over several years, his last day at the Bologna works being in May 1989. Even so, by the time of the Cagiva take-over it was Bordi, rather than Taglioni, who bore the responsibility for designing the latest breed of Ducati for the new era.

THE 750F1

Just as the changeover was taking place (spring 1985), Ducati were constructing the first batches of the new 750F1 street bike. From this came a series of handbuilt customer race replicas for track use or fast road work. These really were 'limited editions', almost to the point of handfuls rather than hundreds being built, and they were more closely related to Villa's F1 racer than to the F1 street bike. Named, depending on the dates they were constructed (1985 through to 1987), Montjuic, Leguna Seca and Santa Monica, these much-loved machines normally had 40mm Dell'Orto PHM carburettors (although a few early Montjuics had 36mm instruments), 10:1 (against the stock bike's 9.3:1) compression pistons, larger valves and a less restrictive exhaust. These special high performance versions made their maximum power in the 7,500–10,000rpm range and transmitted via stock gear clusters, although they had the advantage (like the factory racers) of straight cut, rather than helical cut, primary gears.

Other changes included a square section aluminium swinging arm (as against tubular steel), four-piston Brembo goldline brake calipers (instead of the less powerful two-piston stock type) at the front, and usually slick-type racing rubber. These limited edition F1s could reach 137mph (220km/h), against the works F1 racing model's 145mph (233km/h) plus.

The zenith of the factory TTF1 racer came at Daytona in March 1986, when former GP star and world 500cc champion Marco Lucchinelli won the prestigious Battle of the Twins race on one of the Ducati V-twins.

THE 851

But the really big news – and certainly the real starting point of this chapter – came a year later when Lucchinelli returned to the Florida circuit and won again. But this time it was on a prototype of a very different nature: what was to emerge later as the 851. This latter bike was to play a pivotal role, as the Pantah had done before it, in shaping Ducati's future. The liquid-cooled, fuel-injected, dohc four-valves-per-cylinder, 90-degree, belt-driven V-twin was a huge leap for the Bologna factory. And it was very much the work of Ing. Bordi, with vital input by Franco Farné and Luigi Mengoli.

The very first prototype of what was to later emerge as the 851 series had debuted the year before in the 1986 Bol d'Or 24-hour endurance race. In this event it had been run with a displacement of 750cc; then, redesigned and modified, the bike – still with the 750cc engine size – had been air freighted over the Atlantic to Daytona for the 1987 annual race week. Its performance impressed the press and public alike, with lap times not far off the leading four-cylinder Japanese bikes in the blue riband 200 event. This was the first positive sign of what was to come.

LAUNCH OF WORLD SUPER BIKE

Two major events occurred in 1988. The first was the arrival of the brand new World Super Bike (WSB) race series. The second was the availability of the production 851cc (92 × 64mm) series new V-twin, which customers could buy for the street or track use. And, as if to prove that Ducati treated WSB seriously from the very start, prior to the first round taking place at Donington Park, England, in April 1988, the new factory owners, Cagiva, decided to provide Marco Lucchinelli with a total of no fewer than ten machines and a racing budget that year of around £250,000.

As for the production series, which had made its public debut at the biennial international Milan Show in November 1987, Ducati built a total of 500 examples in the first batch, comprising 300 Strada roaders and 200 851 Kit sports models – the latter to meet homologation requirements governing the WSB series. Full details of the 1988 Strada and Kit models are given in Chapter 3.

Lucchinelli's factory racers were one-offs, weighing in at some 66lb (30kg) lighter than the production models at a slimline 320lb (145kg), down to the bare WSB minimum, taking into account the original strong bias in favour of twins over four-cylinder bikes

Marco Lucchinelli's four-valves-per-cylinder 851-type factory racer on the Ducati stand at the Milan Show in November 1987.

The World Super Bike Championship

The philosophy behind the Super Bike category, which was created half-way through the 1980s, was to race bikes that were very powerful but were similar to production models on sale to the general public. The opportunity for the general public to 'identify' themselves with the bikes that were so close to production models has been the basis for the success of the Super Bike category. The technical regulations, which have remained virtually unchanged since 1988, are a demonstration of the total success of the formula. Four-cylinder bikes up to 750cc, three-cylinder bikes up to 900cc and twin-cylinder mikes up to 1,000cc are all allowed to take part in the championship.

1999 World Super Bike Championship Calendar: Thirteen Rounds

28 Mar	Kyalami	South Africa
18 Apr	Phillip Island	Australia
2 May	Donington Park	Great Britain
16 May	Albacete	Spain
30 May	Monza	Italy
13 Jun	Nurburgring	Germany
27 Jun	Misano Adriatico	San Marino
11 Jul	Laguna Seca	USA
1 Aug	Brands Hatch	Europe
29 Aug	A1-Ring	Austria
5 Sep	Assen	Netherlands
12 Sep	Hockenheim	Germany
10 Oct	Sugo	Japan

regarding minimum weight restrictions. The weight difference between the production roadsters and works racing models was achieved thanks to not just one, but a whole raft of tweaks, including thinner bodywork panels, lighter frame components – notably the tubing itself and special subframes, flywheel and generator – and the dumping of the electric start mechanism, direction indicators and switchgear. The chassis itself was also modified, with taller ride heights at both ends and the fully floating front disc sizes up 40mm to 320mm. Additionally, there were the special engine components needed to bring about a competitive output figure of around 130bhp.

Other important modifications that were rapidly introduced were a move to a larger 888cc (94 × 64mm) displacement (although the bike was still billed an 851) and 17in instead of 16in wheels. During testing the original 1987 851cc-engined prototype (which had itself replaced the earlier 750cc four-valves-per-cylinder prototypes) was timed at 165mph (265km/h); the 1988 Lucchinelli 888cc model probably provided an extra 3–5mph (5–8km/h).

From the 1989 model year Ducati began selling production versions of their factory racers in small quantities, that first year as the Lucchinelli Replica; thereafter (1990 onwards) as the Corsa.

RACING SUCCESS

Although Marco Lucchinelli and Ducati won the first ever WSB race at Donington in 1988, the pairing did not go on to take the title; that particular honour was reserved for the American Fred Merkel, riding a factory Honda RC30 V-four. In truth Ducati used 1988 very much as an extended development test. This allowed Bimota's Davide Tardozzi (later to become manager of the

Ducati Performance team with which Carl Fogarty won the 1998 WSB) to come second in the title race with a Yamaha FZ-engined YB4 four-cylinder. Meanwhile Lucchinelli finished the second race fifth overall.

For 1989 Ducati signed talented Frenchman Raymond Roche, although 'signed' is not really the correct wording, as Roche was already on the books of Cagiva, having ridden for the latter in the 1988 500 Grand Prix series. With Cagiva and Ducati having such close ties, 'in-house transfer' would be a more apt description of the move. The 'Flying Frenchman' went on to achieve an impressive runner-up slot in that year's WSB rankings, behind champion – for a second year – Fred Merkel. However, as Roche had displayed during his first year on a Ducati, the Bologna factory was now ready for its share of the glory. It was now Ducati, rather than Honda, who was in charge.

Roche was again the number one Ducati man for 1990, except that he exchanged the runner-up spot for the championship winner's laurels. The former Bimota rider Giancarlo Falappa also made his mark, riding a Ducati for the first time as an official factory entry that year. The crowds loved his spectacular (although crash-prone) style. Even today he's one of Ducati's favourite names with the fans, even though he was forced to retire after a horrendous injury several years ago.

By now Honda had been joined by both Kawasaki and Yamaha, and the WSB pace was hotting up.

Technically, Ducati at last had machinery that was not only super quick, but reliable too. And it was this combination that gave Roche and the Italian factory their first WSB title.

For 1991 Ducati started the season strong favourites after their championship victory the previous year. This optimism proved well founded with not only Roche and Falappa,

Raymond Roche's 1989 factory bike, the year before he became Ducati's first WSB champion in 1990.

The Italian round of the World Super Bike series at Monza, 7 October 1990. The soon-to-be-crowned champion Raymond Roche (Ducati) is number 3, in the centre on the front row.

Close-up view of Roche's 1990 championship winner, as the rider saw things.

(Below) *To celebrate their first WSB Championship Ducati produced this signed sticker (below) of their new hero, Frenchman Raymond Roche. Today the sticker is a valuable collector's piece.*

but also the American Doug Polen joining the ranks of the thundering red twins from Bologna. It was Polen who went on to garner Ducati's second WSB title – making it a third the following year just to prove what a stranglehold Ducati now exercised on the class.

Doug Polen seemed to come and go quickly. Whilst he was around he was rarely beaten, but although he won two world titles, he returned to his native America rather too quickly. He may well have decided to quit while he was ahead, as the competition was getting ever hotter, or maybe after two world titles he didn't feel hungry in the same way as before – or perhaps he just got homesick. But there is no doubt that whilst he was around, in 1991 and 1992, Doug Polen did much to establish Ducati's reputation on both sides of the Atlantic.

With Polen quitting the squad, Falappa injured and Roche retired, Ducati signed Englishman Carl Fogarty (whose father George, interestingly, had ridden the old bevel V-twins for Sports Motorcycles during the late 1970s). Carl Fogarty from Blackburn, Lancashire, had first come into the Ducati frame in the summer of 1992, when he created a sensation at the Donington Park round by soundly beating the entire works teams (not just Ducati, but Kawasaki and Honda as well) on a privately entered 888 Corsa production bike. With Kawasaki in particular getting ever more competitive, Ducati's engineering team introduced a larger displacement motor for 1993. With the 926cc (96×64mm) unit, Fogarty took no fewer than eleven WSB race victories. But with the title going to the final round, he eventually

(Above) *One of the 1991-type racers on display at an Italian exhibition that year. It is actually Davide Tardozzi's European Championship-winning bike, hence the number one plate. Tardozzi later became team manager for the Ducati Performance squad.*

Runner-up in 1989, Raymond Roche's championship victory in 1990 triggered a whole series of Ducati titles in the class.

This fairing-off shot reveals considerable detail on one of the 1991 factory machines as campaigned by the likes of Roche, Polen and Falappa that year.

The dry clutch with its carbon-fibre cover. Also evident in this view are the cam drive belts and magnesium engine cover.

The Milan Show, November 1991: American Doug Polen's world championship-winning 888cc Ducati with its bodywork removed.

(Below right) Giancarlo Falappa, never a world champion, but still one of the most popular Ducati riders ever. He is seen here in 1992 in his familiar aggressive style.

(Below) Until 1991 Doug Polen was simply an American who raced big-bore Japanese bikes in the AMA (American Motorcycle Association) championships. The turning point in his career came thanks to Eraldo Ferracci (Fast by Ferracci) who sent him to Europe. So impressed were Ducati that they added Polen to their list of officially supported riders, which for 1991 consisted of Roche, Falappa and Mertens. The American proved his worth by not only taking the 1991 title, but winning the 1992 one as well, before returning to the USA.

(Above) *How the other half lives. Virginio Ferrari (centre, former racer and one of Ducati's team managers) and his engineering staff relax during qualifying week for one of the WSB rounds in 1994.*

Carl Fogarty during his early days as a Ducati rider in 1993, when he rode for the British importers Moto Cinelli.

finished runner-up to Kawasaki's American rider, Scott Russell.

INTRODUCTION OF THE 916

The following year – 1994 – was of course the year of the sensational 916. The two men most notably involved in its development were Ing. Massimo Bordi at Ducati and Massimo Tamburini at CRC (Cagiva Research Centre).

A central feature of the 916 was its ram-air induction system, which had already been tried and tested on Cagiva's 500 GP two-stroke four-cylinder racer, and the single-

To make the 851 more accessible Ducati introduced the Superbike 851 Monoposto (single seat) for the 1989 model year to replace the 1988 Tricolore Strada and Kit versions.

Marco Lucchinelli during the first year of WSB (World Super Bike) racing, 1988.

(Left) *Ing. Massimo Bordi was the man behind the creation of the four-valves-per-cylinder, liquid-cooled, dohc, fuel-injection 90-degree Desmo V-twin engine.*

The four-valve head has created a whole family of Ducati motorcycles that have made their own legend in just over a decade.

(Below) *Italian rider Mario Lucchiari in action during the WSB round at Brands Hatch, circa 1992. The bike is a works-supported 888cc Corsa.*

(Above) *The top-of-the-range 888 SPS of 1992, only 100 of which were built. The styling was identical to the SP4 of the same era, but with carbon-fibre silencers and fuel tank. There was also a 1991-spec Corsa engine. In other words, the SPS was virtually a race bike and came with a race radiator, which had no cooling fan.*

Much of the design work, including the styling, chassis and ram-air system for the 916 was done at the Cagiva Research Centre (CRC) by Massimo Tamburini (left) and Massimo Parenti.

(Below) *First shown at the end of 1993, the new 916 was a sensation, having a greater impact than probably any sports motorcycle of the 1990s. Deliveries began in May 1994. This is the original Monoposto (single seat) model.*

Before his untimely death in the summer of 1994, Ayrton Senna had reached agreement with Cagiva supremo Claudio Castiglioni for a motorcycle bearing his name to be produced. The 916 Senna was built in three batches, each of 300 units. The Series I arrived in 1995, the Series II and III coming in 1997 and 1998 respectively.

To many the 748 (a 1995 SP is shown) is even better than the 916, with its revvier engine and pin-sharp handling characteristics.

(Above) *American GP star Jon Kocinski rode for Ducati in the 1996 WSB series. His main sponsor was Kremlyovskaya Vodka. By now the engine size had grown to 996cc.*

Another foreign Ducati star was Australian Troy Corser, pictured here at Brands Hatch on 4 August 1996. After finishing runner-up to Carl Fogarty in 1995 he became world champion at the end of the 1996 season.

(Above) *New for the 1997 model year, the 916 SPS had a 996cc (98 × 66mm) engine size and was closely related to the Corsa over-the-counter racing machine.*

Multiple world champion Carl Fogarty at the launch of the Ducati Performance racing school at Brands Hatch, 25 February 1998.

(Below) *The final year of production for the 916 series machines was 1998. Shown here is a Biposto (dual seat) model from the last production batch that year.*

(Right) *British importer Moto Cinelli's workshop manager Iain Rhodes checking over a 916-series machine at the company's Northampton headquarters in August 1998.*

(Left) *A 1998 916 SPS (actual engine displacement 996cc) under test that year. It was the forerunner to the even more specialized Foggy Replica.*

(Below) *The Foggy Replica tested by the author in August 1998. To quote a* Motor Cycle News *test: 'Those lucky few who will be able to flash their special Foggy Replica key fobs down the pub may have to fork out a fortune but they can at least boast they own the flashiest Ducati road bike ever built!'*

(Above) *Carl Fogarty's 1998 World Super Bike Championship-winning 996cc works Ducati with technical details on view.*

(Below) *New for 1999, the ST4 sports-tourer added a new dimension to the four-valve V-twin story. It also gave Ducati a whole new clientele to aim for in their goal to increase their market share.*

sided swinging arm, which was an entirely new feature, for Ducati at any rate. Another vital change was the engine's displacement, which was upped to 955cc (96 × 66mm).

The 916-style, 955cc-engined 1994 works racer also featured a one-off 'slipper clutch'. This worked as follows. While downshifting under braking, the clutch slipped slightly to prevent the rear wheel locking up and thus hopping or sliding around.

Testing Carl Fogarty's 1995 bike, former Grand Prix star Niall Mackenzie said: 'The bike already has loads of engine braking. This and the slipper clutch are a superb combination. Without that clutch the rear wheel goes sideways. I reckon Foggy's slipper clutch is worth about a second a lap on its own.'

Other alterations compared with the over-the-counter Corsa customer racers included changes to the exhaust system, flywheel and camshafts, and titanium exhaust valves;

Carl Fogarty testing one of the new 916-type factory racers in early 1994 (at Donington Park). The actual capacity of 955cc was also new for that season.

plus a totally different chip for the computer. Mackenzie, who also tested a Corsa to provide a comparison between the two bikes, went on to reveal:

> On the Corsa, the engine has to be at 8,500rpm before it pulls hard. But on Foggy's bike the power is there, ready to use, at 6,000 revs. At higher revs, the bike feels no stronger than a Corsa. From 10,000 revs, Carl's bike doesn't make any more power than the Corsa and the rev limiter comes in at about 11,700 – just the same. The Corsa is 955cc – the same as Foggy's. But as his bike has so much low-down grunt, it feels like a 10,000!

With Fogarty joining the Virginio Ferrari Ducati team for 1994, Moto Cinelli signed James Whitham to compete in both the British and WSB championship series that year. Whitham proved a popular choice, and also won the Indonesian round of the world series.

(Below) James Whitham's 955cc factory Ducati V-twin, on which he was victorious in the 1994 Indonesian WSB round.

(Above) *The World Super Bike grid at Mugello, Italy, in the summer of 1994. This photograph captures the almost Formula 1 car-type professionalism of motorbike racing today.*

Carl Fogarty at speed in 1994, the first year the Englishman won the WSB title for Ducati. The number two plate relates to the previous year, when he finished runner-up to Kawasaki's Scott Russell.

(Above) *Three important Ducati figures together in 1994, from left to right: Marco Lucchinelli, Hoss Elm (British Ducati importer) and Virginio Ferrari.*

(Below) *A WSB round in 1995, world champion Carl Fogarty leading from Arran Slight (Honda), Troy Corser (Ducati) and another four riders.*

A 1995 banner from Foggy supporters in 1995 reads: 'We're following Foggy just like Russell, Slight, Corser, Crafer, Chilli, Gobert and Pirovano.'

(Below) A Ducati race transporter from the WSB squad outside the Bologna factory, summer 1995.

A 1,000cc BIKE

Up to now Ducati had never made full use of the WSB rule book, which allowed for a maximum engine displacement of 1,000cc for twins, 900cc for triples and 750cc for four cylinders. In the early days the Italian factory did not need a full displacement to make a successful challenge, but as time went by, the sports governing body slowly took away the weight restrictions that the four-cylinder models had to carry compared to the twins. And so came the ultimate leap to 1,000cc. The Ducati engineering team achieved this feat not by upping the bore, but by adding instead an extra 2mm to the stroke, thus giving a new capacity of 996cc.

At the end of 1995, after his second consecutive WSB title, Carl Fogarty, deciding he needed a new challenge, joined Honda. *Ducatisti* around the world were stunned. I well remember the day the news reached the fans at the British Motorcycle Show at the NEC Birmingham in November 1995: they were aghast, as were all the vendors with Fogarty/Ducati merchandise! Why quit a winning squad, fans asked? To be fair, Foggy did feel he needed to prove he could win on something other than a Ducati. There was also a nice, fat cheque from Honda, which must have helped too …

But in the event it proved a bad move for the 'Blackburn Bullet', as racing a Honda meant riding the previously less-than-successful RC45 V-four (the successor to the same company's RC30). It did not take Fogarty long to start having doubts about the wisdom of his switch. And in due course he told everyone, via the column of *Motor Cycle News*: 'I wish I had remained at Ducati'. Even though he managed a couple of excellent results at Hockenheim in Germany and Assen in Holland, Foggy could only watch as his championship title slowly slipped away, with his former team-mate, Australian Troy Corser, winning it for Ducati.

With big changes at Ducati (the Texas Pacific buy-in took place in September 1996) there was at last a much-needed injection of new capital into the Bologna company (*see* Chapter 9). Again, when one considers the state of Ducati's finances during the previous year it perhaps should not be such a shock that Fogarty had taken the safe route to financial security by signing for Honda … With the need to win and secure a future employer Fogarty went back to Ducati in another well-publicized deal. *Motor Cycle News* reported: 'the 30-year-old has been lured back by a £250,000 pay rise and the prospect of riding the bike he took to the WSB title in 1994 and '95.' At around the same time Jon Kocinski, who had raced for Ducati in 1996, joined Honda.

RETURN OF FOGGY

But if Fogarty and Ducati thought it was to be an immediate happy homecoming, they were both to be proved wrong, even though the first half of the 1997 season was to finish with Foggy narrowly ahead of his American rival Kocinski. But it was plain to see that for the first time the Honda RC45 was a serious threat. In addition Fogarty could not rely on backing from Corser, as the Australian had left to try his hand in Grand Prix!

The second half of the 1997 WSB season was to prove a bitter one for the Englishman as he was to see his lead in the championship disappear. Everyone had expected that it would be the temperamental Kocinski who would crack under pressure, but instead it was more often than not Fogarty. A typical occasion was the European round at Brands Hatch. In front of his home fans Foggy crashed out of the first race, then in a two-part second leg (caused by rain) he

Troy Corser

The naturally talented Australian champion Troy Corser is one of the fastest and most spectacular riders in World Super Bike today. A WSB title in 1996, thirteen wins and sixteen pole positions are the hallmarks of his success with the twin-cylinder Italian bike. Seven pole positions in twelve races in the 1998 season are a superb demonstration of his determination and will to win.

Troy Corser was born on 27 November 1971 at Wollongong, New South Wales, and entered his first race at the age of ten in the Enduro category.

Australian Troy Corser, the 1996 World Super Bike champion on his way to another victory that season. His race number did not do him justice!

Career

1981	Enduro racing at age of ten	
1986–88	Motocross and dirt-track	
1989	First track race at Oran Park (Sydney)	(Honda CR125)
1990	Australian 250 Production Champion	
1990	16th Australian 250 Championship	
1992	4th Australian Super Bike Championship	(Yamaha)
1993	Australian Super Bike Champion	(Honda)
1994	AMA American Super Bike Champion (First non-American to win title)	(Ducati)
1995	2nd World Super Bike Championship	(Ducati)
1996	World Super Bike Champion	(Ducati)
1997	World 500 Championship	(Yamaha)
1998	3rd World Super Bike Championship	(Ducati)

stuck his neck out when he didn't need to in the re-run to prove a point to the crowd.

At the end of the season, with Kocinski champion and Foggy runner-up, it was generally agreed that the Ducati man had lost the title, rather than that Kocinski had won it. Quite simply, Carl had failed to finish too often, mostly as the result of accidents. Looking back behind the bare results sheets it was pretty evident that Foggy had very often been trying *too* hard to win. In retrospect (always easy after the event) he should perhaps have followed the 'points make prizes' route, rather than the 'win at all costs' one.

However, things are seldom quite as simple as this. Besides Fogarty's 'lionheart' will to win there was another problem, which meant that Ducati themselves were to make a mistake that was to affect Fogarty's 1997 championship bid.

Since 1994 the FIM had added an additional 15kg (33lb) to the weight limit allowed for the twins, whilst the four-cylinder bikes had been able to dispense with 5kg (11lb) – making in effect an additional weight penalty for Ducati, compared to its Japanese four-cylinder rivals. In Ducati's case this additional weight was the cause of the problem.

The Paddock Hill Bend Grandstand at Brands Hatch, the top place to be for spectators during the World Super Bike European round. Currently Britain effectively has two rounds, the other (British) round being staged at Donington Park.

Back in 1995, when Fogarty last rode for Ducati, the weight penalty was addressed simply by placing lead weights on the bike in whatever position the particular rider requested. Troy Corser put his on the headstock, Fogarty on the rear of the frame. In 1996 Corser had won the title, then left to chase GP glory (which did not happen).

When Fogarty rejoined Ducati for the 1997 season, Ducati also suffered the loss of one of its most influential race engineers Ivo Bertoni, who, through seven successful seasons (from Roche's initial 1990 championship to Corser's in 1996), had played a vital role. Very much the unsung hero, Ivo Bertoni was a man who really was in the business for the love of the sport, rather than for any financial gain (his father was a wealthy industrialist who owned a vast factory complex making earth-moving equipment). Bertoni left Ducati after the end of the 1996 season to help run the family business. This led to new engineers being brought in to replace this important man, but they were not only outsiders, they also had their own ideas and felt it necessary to stamp their own authority.

The result was a number of largely unreported (by the press) changes to the factory racing team bikes. An example of this was a newly designed fuel tank, which not only altered the riding position but also the weight distribution. In addition, during 1996, the practice of adding lead weights to the frame was replaced by incorporating these weights into the design of the motorcycle itself. This meant a new chassis was introduced, which was provided with the front end bias favoured by Troy Corser. Unfortunately when Corser left and Fogarty rejoined the team, the Englishman's preference for rearward weight distribution was overlooked ...

The result was that Fogarty was to campaign a bike, which, in his own words, 'didn't handle as well as my 1995 machine'. Anyone who was there at the meetings (or even on video tape) was able to see that Fogarty's

The 996 Factory Racer (1998)

Engine	Liquid-cooled 90-degree V-twin four-stroke
Displacement	996cc
Bore and stroke	98 × 66mm
Timing system	4 valves per cylinder
Fuel system	Electronic injection
Injection-ignition	Magneti Marelli
Final drive	Regina chain
Brake horsepower	163bhp at 11,500rpm
Gearbox	6 speeds
Clutch	Dry, hydraulic control
Frame	Steel trestle
Front suspension	Öhlins upside-down fork
Rear suspension	Magnesium swing arm, Öhlins single shock absorber
Front brakes	Brembo 2 × 320/290mm, Brembo 4-piston calipers
Rear brake	Brembo 1 × 200mm, Brembo 2-piston caliper
Tyres	Michelin
Length	80in (2,030mm)
Width	27in (685mm)
Wheelbase	56in (1,430mm)
Dry weight	357lb (162kg)
Fuel tank capacity	24 litres (5.25imp. gal)
Top speed	187mph (300km/h)

In one of the most dramatic finishes to a season ever witnessed in two-wheel sport Carl Fogarty took his Team Ducati Performance 996 to a hugely popular WSB title.

The fairing panels removed to show engine and frame details of Fogarty's 1998 championship winner. It is reputed that each factory 996 racer costs a cool £200,000 to build.

The engine from Fogarty's 1998 World Super Bike-winning 996cc Ducati V-twin.

At Assen in Holland (in September 1998) the rivalry between Fogarty and Chilli boiled over after the former won and the latter fell following a race-long duel that was only resolved at the last corner of the last lap. Foggy is handed the English flag after his victory.

1997 bike was a wayward beast – and his aggressive will to win only made things worse. In my view it was the front weight bias of the new chassis that really lost Fogarty the 1997 title!

But in a strange way the problems of 1997 were to play into Fogarty's hands during 1998, when he rode with his head, rather than his heart. Some may say his dramatic championship victory of 1998 was luck – but

Fogarty (2) leads fellow Ducati rider Pier Francisco Chilli (7) at Druids Corner, Brands Hatch, in August 1998. The competition was intense between the two all year, even though they were riding for the same factory.

in racing you make your own luck, and Fogarty let the others (Corser and Slight) make the mistakes this time. He had learned the hard way, but been man enough to realize what he had done wrong the previous year, and put it right – the sign of a true champion and master of his sport. Furthermore, after

his disastrous move to Honda for the 1996 season Fogarty was not about to make the same mistake again and now looks set to see out his racing career with the Italian marque.

Another consideration is that for 1997 Fogarty came under the wing of the team manager Davide Tardozzi, who managed the

Carl Fogarty (right) relaxes with supporters after yet another hard-earned victory. His 1998 world title must go down as the most exciting in the history of the sport.

Davide Tardozzi, Team Manager 1999

Team Ducati Performance, Super Bike and Super Sport, is run by Davide Tardozzi. His twenty-year career as rider and team manager give him enormous experience in the world of motorcycle racing. Within Ducati Corse Davide Tardozzi holds another fundamental position in addition to sporting director. He is responsible for supervision and contacts with all riders of the official teams, as well as 'special observer' of young talent in whom to invest in the future.

Davide Tardozzi was born in Ravenna on 30 January 1959. He won five Italian championships and a European title, as well as four World Super Bike Championship races. As team manager, he won two World Super Bike titles, in 1996 with Troy Corser and in 1998 with Carl Fogarty.

World Super Bike Championship Winners

1988	Fred Merkel	USA	Honda
1989	Fred Merkel	USA	Honda
1990	Raymond Roche	FRA	Ducati 851
1991	Doug Polen	USA	Ducati 888
1992	Doug Polen	USA	Ducati 888
1993	Scott Russell	USA	Kawasaki
1994	Carl Fogarty	UK	Ducati 916
1995	Carl Fogarty	UK	Ducati 916
1996	Troy Corser	AUS	Ducati 916
1997	Jon Kocinski	USA	Honda
1998	Carl Fogarty	UK	Ducati 996

**Team Ducati Performance,
1999 WSB Championship**

Team Manager
Davide Tardozzi

Riders
Carl Fogarty
Troy Corser

Chief Engineer, Ducati Corse
Corrado Cecchinelli

Carl Fogarty Technical Crew

Luca Gasbarro	Track engineer, Ducati Corse
Matthew Casey	Electronics engineer
Anthony Bass	Chief mechanic
Paul Hallet	Mechanic
Guglielmo Andreini	Mechanic
Filippo Farina	Mechanic

Troy Corser Technical Crew

Roberto Bonazzi	Track engineer, Ducati Corse
Luca Minelli	Electronics engineer
Bruno Leoni	Chief mechanic
Andrea Bonassoli	Mechanic
Roberto Clerici	Mechanic
Giorgio Casturà	Mechanic

Technical Components
Maurizio Perlini

Suspension Engineer
Jon Cornwell   Öhlins

Engineer
Philippe Louche   Michelin

Brake Systems Engineer
Franco Zonnedda   Brembo

Press Officer
Michele Morisetti, Ducati Corse

Hospitality and PR
Paola Braiato, Ducati Corse

Photographer
Fabrizio Porrozzi

Team Ducati Performance, which was new that year. This combination not only proved successful, but Ducati's management realized just how successful by deciding to run *only* one team for 1999 and that was Team Ducati Performance, with only two riders, Fogarty and Corser. On paper this really does seem a 'dream team', the two riders having taken no fewer than four WSB titles between them over the preceding five years.

**Ducati Race Victories in the
World Super Bike Championship
(to 1 January 1999)**

Wins	Rider	Nationality
44	Carl Fogarty	UK
26	Doug Polen	USA
23	Raymond Roche	France
13	Giancarlo Falappa	Italy
13	Troy Corser	Australia
11	Pier Francesco Chilli	Italy
5	Jon Kocinski	USA
2	Mario Lucchiari	Italy
2	Marco Lucchinelli	Italy
2	Stephane Mertens	Belgium
1	James Whitham	UK
1	Andreas Meklau	Austria

In the fierce competition that is today's World Super Bike racing, the backroom engineering team behind Ducati's success is all important. Yes, you must have the top riders, but in road racing, as against off-road events, like motocross or trials, the machine *has* to match or beat the opposition to win. So development is continuous: what was good a few months, or in some cases, weeks ago, is not good enough today. As an example, the frame on the Ducati 996 racer was modified after the 1998 season had got under way; the reason was quite simple – a new airbox had been developed that allowed the engine to breathe better and give more mid-range power. As for

The Foggy Interview

Foggy flies in for the interview session.

Mick Walker (left) interviews Carl Fogarty, Monday 15 March 1999, prior to the defence of his WSB Championship title.

MW *From the last time we met [November 1995] you seem to be much more relaxed and comfortable with yourself in public.*

CF Yes, this is correct. I think that having a settled team has helped, also my manager, Davide Tardozzi, has played an important part in this.

MW *There have been rumours concerning your possible retirement now that you have won three WSB titles.*

CF I will continue racing as long as I still enjoy it. Don't believe everything you see in the press. At present I'm going out there to retain the title in 1999, but who knows from one year to another.

MW *You received a big offer to switch to Suzuki, how near did you come to making the switch?*

CF Well, after my Honda experience, and that I'm now in a settled team, I have decided to stay with Ducati. It's also a bike that suits my particular riding style.

MW *This year you have Troy Corser as a team-mate, rather than simply someone who is riding for the same factory, but in a different squad. Do you see Troy as a rival or friend?*

CF Friend when we are not out on the track. Obviously both of us want to win when we are racing. I don't know Troy that well, but we get on okay.

MW *What does your wife Mikala think of you racing?*

CF We met before I started racing, in fact in our schooldays. I think I'm really lucky as I know she wants me for myself, not my money. I would hate to be someone like Max Biaggi – as he's unmarried he never knows if someone's after him or his fame.

MW *What don't you like?*

CF When I'm out with the wife shopping and someone wants to drag me over to meet all his friends.

MW *Do you currently have a road bike?*

CF No, but if I did it would probably be a Monster, equally good for touring or a bit of fun.

Carl in characteristic pose.

the frame, this was only modified so the new airbox could be fitted, the basic geometry staying the same. No doubt as you are read-ing this yet more updates are being tested and incorporated into the basic design to keep Ducati at the top.

The 1999 AMA American Super Bike Championship

When the Super Bike category was born in the United States the result in terms of spectator attedance and sale of production bikes was extraordinary. Success in this championship is there-fore a decisive factor in commercial results.

Ducati have always played a leading role in the AMA series, winning the title in 1993 and 1994. In 1999 they will be taking part in the AMA American Super Bike Championship with two official facto-ry-assisted teams: Vance & Hines, run by Terry Vance, and Fast by Ferracci, run by the Italo-Amercan Eraldo Ferracci.

The two teams will be racing the 1999 version of the Ducati 996 Factory in the AMA series and will be directly supported by specialized technical personnel sent from Ducati Corse to the USA.

Riders

Vance & Hines Team	Anthony Gobert and Ben Bostrom
Fast by Ferracci Team	Matt Wait

The 1999 AMA Super Bike Championship has a thirteen-event calendar, making a total of fourteen rounds, owing to the double-header event at Road Atlanta on 5/6 June.

1999 AMA Super Bike Championship Calendar

7 Mar	Daytona Beach	FL	Daytona Int. Speedway
21 Mar	Phoenix	AZ	Phoenix Int. Raceway
18 Apr	Rosamund	CA	Willow Spring Int. Speedway
25 Apr	Sonoma	CA	Seas Point Raceway
2 May	Monterey	CA	Laguna Seca Raceway
6 Jun	Braselton	GA	Road Atlanta (2 races)
13 Jun	Elkhart Lake	WI	Road America
20 Jun	Loudon	NH	New Hampshire Int. Speedway
11 Jul	Monterey	CA	Laguna Seca WSBK
18 Jul	Lexington	OH	Mid-Ohio Sports Car Course
1 Aug	Brainerd	MN	Brainerd Int. Raceway
19 Sep	Fountain	CO	Pike's Peak Int. Raceway
3 Oct	Las Vegas	NV	Las Vegas Motor Speedway

AMA American Super Bike Championship Winners

1992	Scott Russell	USA	Kawasaki
1993	Doug Polen	USA	Ducati
1994	Troy Corser	AUS	Ducati
1995	Miguel DuHamel	USA	Honda
1996	Doug Chandler	USA	Kawasaki
1997	Doug Chandler	USA	Kawasaki
1998	Ben Bostrom	USA	Honda

9 Political Events

Ducati, or at least their motorcycle arm, seem to have been perpetually involved in what we will describe as political controversy.

When the Ducati motorcycle celebrated its fiftieth anniversary in 1998 it could look back upon half a century of not only some remarkable achievements but also a roller-coaster ride of financial stability alternating with dire financial problems down through the years.

As Chapter 1 reveals, Ducati as a corporate grouping was rescued at the end of the Second World War after their production facilities had virtually ceased to exist after sustained Allied bombing raids, which became a fact of life in northern Italy towards the end of the hostilities.

POST-WAR EXPANSION

Ducati's first foray into the world of the wheels had come with the Cucciolo (Little Pup). Designed by Turin-based lawyer Aldo Farinelli, the Cucciolo micro-engine was used to power a wide range of what today would be described as mopeds, but over half a century ago were usually referred to as cyclemotors – the engine literally being attached to what amounted to little more than a pedal cycle frame, but with a 'clip-on' device.

At that time Ducati was only able to manufacture the Cucciolo and subsequent small capacity motorcycles because of a joint venture by the Italian government and, of all people, the Vatican in Rome.

Then in 1953 Ducati was split into two separate companies: Ducati Meccanica, responsible for everything mechanical – motorcycles, stationary engines, marine engines and later diesel engines for automobiles – and Ducati Elettrotecnica (the electrical side of the original business). The two separate concerns were housed alongside each other in production facilities in the Borgo Panigale area of downtown Bologna. With Ing. Fabio Taglioni joining in May 1954, Ducati Meccanica at last had a designer of world-class ability. The other key figure during the 1950s was Doctor Giuseppe Montano, chief executive from the early 1950s until removed at the end of the 1960s. And its was these two men who between them established Ducati as a motorcycle manufacturer whose products were sold around the world.

Like other motorcycle concerns, Ducati was able to expand rapidly during the first half of the 1950s – when it was very much a seller's market. The appointment of Ing. Taglioni allowed this progress to continue when many of Ducati's major rivals, such as Moto Guzzi and Gilera, were struggling during the latter half of that decade. In fact, when FB Mondial, Moto Guzzi and Gilera quit Grand Prix racing in a tripartite pact at the end of 1957, Ducati stepped forward to challenge Count Dominico Agusta's mighty MV squad in the 1958 125cc world championship series with

Taglioni's masterful Desmo single.

Ducati, with their range of exciting new overhead cam roadster models (including 125, 175 and 200cc versions) and a new Desmo twin, seemed poised for success on both the showroom and racing stages as the decade drew to a close. But it was not to be. Quite simply the combination of development costs for the newly created Taglioni-designed bikes for both street and circuit had depleted the company's cash reserves. The result was a virtual withdrawal from racing and a severe belt-tightening exercise – the first of many such incidents – and a warning that was not fully heeded at the time. Dr Montano managed to turn things around during the early 1960s, helped in no small measure by steadily increasing export sales, notably to the USA.

The laurel wreath Ducati Meccanica logo as used during the late 1950s, one of the most colourful ever to grace a motorcycle.

CRISIS IN THE 60S AND 70S

By a cruel twist of fate it was this very success that was to bring about Ducati's next crisis, during late 1966, when the American distributors, the New Jersey-based Berliner Corporation misjudged the market and were left with a warehouse full of unsold machines. This was to result in a whole shipload of Stateside-style Ducatis being dumped on the British market; the ship itself simply found its New York destination changed to Liverpool. And for Berliner read Bill Hannah, a wily Scot who was involved in a number of businesses at the time. The rerouted American shipment totalled some 3,500 machines and took some four years to sell into a depressed UK market. This event did nothing to foster good relationships between Ducati and Berliner, or for that matter with the British importers of the time, Vic Camp.

With a rapidly worsening financial crisis at Ducati Meccanica, the Italian company, who had years previously taken over the Vatican's remaining shareholding, was forced to take extreme measures to stave off a financial meltdown. The first of these was to appoint the government body EFIM as a holding company, the second was to dispense with the services of Dr Montano, who had engineered most of the factory's success (and occasional failures) during the previous twenty years.

In the short term there can be no doubt that the sacking of Dr Montano and the EFIM appointment led Ducati away from the abyss. This move also had the huge bonus of directly leading to the design concept that would be the cornerstone of the marque's very future, the 90-degree V-twin.

Following this management shake-up, 1969 saw newcomers Arnaldo Milvio and Fredmano Spairani take over as joint bosses of the reorganized Ducati Meccanica SpA. It was this pair's conviction that the next decade would see a trend towards bigger machines (remember that the groundbreaking four-cylinder Honda CB750 was launched in 1969!), and so, encouraged by Ing. Taglioni's obvious enthusiasm for the

Cagiva, owned by the Castiglioni family, took over the former Aermacchi-Harley-Davidson motorcycle factory in Varese during the summer of 1978. They started by constructing road and trail bikes based on the lightweight HD two-strokes, such as this SST125.

L-shaped V-twin engine, Ducati took this new path.

Even so, the Milvio and Spairani team had one major flaw – they ended up spending more money than they made! So once again, in late 1972, Ducati faced another financial crisis. This resulted in yet more changes – a newly constructed factory (already begun under Milvio and Spairani) on the same site as the original, the decision to scrap the entire range of classic bevel singles; the replacement of the 750 bevel V-twin range by a new slab-sided 860GT (engine by Taglioni, styling by the Giugiaro-owned Ital Design studio (who had penned the original Mark I VW Golf)), a new single-cylinder off-road two-stroke and finally a range of chain-drive overhead parallel twins in an (unsuccessful!) attempt to outdo the Japanese at their own game.

Sure enough, the Rome-based nameless government officials who dreamed up this bizarre 'grand plan' got it horribly wrong. Only in-house projects such as the 900SS and Darmah saved the day.

Now known as Gruppo EFIM, Ducati's controllers somehow continued to extract yet more money from the Italian government to

(Above) *By the early 1980s Cagiva had not only established themselves as the top-selling marque in the all-important Italian domestic market, but had begun to build world class off-road motocross (a WMX125 is illustrated here) and enduro bikes.*

The Castiglioni brothers Gianfranco and Claudio were also great road-racing enthusiasts, and thus began a hyper-expensive exercise to develop a world-beating 500cc GP bike. This is one of the first efforts with Virginio Ferrari aboard, circa 1982.

prop up the loss-making bike arm. No doubt, if the diesel and marine engines had not been doing quite nicely, Ducati would have gone belly-up there and then.

At the start of the 1980s Ducati Meccanica came under another government umbrella, in the shape of the Finmeccanica-funded VM Group. By now sales of Ducati's excellent diesel automobile engines to the likes of Alfa Romeo and British Leyland (Rover) was the only real source of income. Ducati as a bike builder was dying on its feet.

ENTER CAGIVA

June 1983 brought the shock announcement (but of no surprise to insiders) that the then little-known Cagiva motorcycle company would in future be buying the bulk of Ducati's motorcycle engines for fitment into machines of their own design (the Allazura and Elefant are notable examples). Rumours abounded that this was the end of Ducati. Of course the press got it all wrong. In reality it was the start of something big.

Then came a period of news blackout from both Ducati and Cagiva, which was only really finally broken with an official statement on the 1 May 1985 that Cagiva had purchased Ducati. It was later to transpire that in the preceding two decades Ducati had made a profit in only one of those years!

Cagiva was a private company and instantly set about a modernization programme. In fact the gap between June 1983 and May 1985 had largely been taken up with the Castiglioni brothers, Gianfranco and Claudio, extracting as much government support for their intended purchase of Ducati as possible. At least one source claims this eventually came to as much as a staggering 70 per cent of the purchase price! In other words the Italian government almost paid Cagiva to buy Ducati. Of course this sort of scenario is

not unique to Italy. One has only to remind British readers, for example, of a very similar situation where the government did virtually the same thing, 'selling' off the ailing British Leyland (Rover) to British Aerospace. And Cagiva, like British Aerospace, were eventually to benefit further from a sale to a third party…

At first Ducati came under the umbrella of Cagiva Commerciale SpA. After purchasing various other companies (including Moto Morini, Husqvarna, the licence rights to the Mini Moke four-wheeler and a large slice of the Czech CZ concern) the holding

Cagiva's initial commercial involvement with Ducati began in June 1983, with an agreement to use the Pantah series engine in a new range of larger-capacity Cagiva motorcycles. The full union occurred on 1 May 1985, when Cagiva purchased Ducati from the Italian government. The Cagiva elephant motif soon made its way into the Ducati lifestyle.

Claudio Castiglioni, the younger of the two brothers, was the driving force in Cagiva's rebuilding of Ducati between 1985 and the Texas Pacific buy-in of 1996.

company subsequently changed its title to Cagiva Trading SpA.

By the early 1990s Cagiva (and Ducati) seemed to be on a roll. In fact just the reverse was true – the money was running out. The reasons are many and varied but two major ones stand out. Firstly, the Castiglionis spent lavishly to satisfy their burning desire to see a Cagiva win a 500cc World title. The second factor was the scandal that rocked Italian political circles brought about by the very same hand-outs that had helped the Castiglionis build up their business empire – government-assisted 'grants'.

When the superb new 916 finally went on sale in the spring of 1994 deliveries were late and not enough machines were available. At the time all sorts of excuses were dished up, but the real truth was that Ducati, or more accurately their owners, Cagiva, were in trouble, big trouble.

By the end of 1995 things had reached such a point that not only were parts suppliers not being paid, but factory employees were only working part time. All this meant was that fewer motorcycles were available and there was a vast backlog of unfulfilled orders. It was also becoming public knowledge that something serious was amiss. Behind the scenes a little-known fact is that auto giants Fiat were even providing management assistance. As for the Castiglionis, they were by now actively seeking outside investors, with America as their number one target.

TEXAS PACIFIC GROUP AND THE END OF THE CASTIGLIONI ERA

One of the first potential investors to be mentioned in the press was the Chicago-based financier Sam Zell, who, because of his personal collection of Ducati motorcycles, was a particularly visible entity. But contrary to the press stories that were circulating in early 1996 around the USA in particular, the Cagiva Group never actually entered into an agreement with the Zell Chilmark Fund and their banking underwriters, Merrill Lynch. In fact, in an exclusive interview with journalist Alan Cathcart in February 1996, Claudio Castiglioni stated:

> It is quite untrue that we made any deal with him, and we are unhappy about the reports that come from his side saying that we have, because we are all concerned that this will give the wrong impression to other companies we're negotiating with, and perhaps discourage them from continuing talks.

And there were several financial groups interested in what was seen, in the US at least, as a blue-chip investment opportunity.

By August 1996 a deal had been thrashed out, but not before the two Castiglioni brothers had themselves disagreed, to such an extent that at one stage the whole plan almost collapsed. Claudio Castiglioni had

Based in Varese on the shores of Lake Como, the Cagiva factory carries a reminder of its past as an aviation plant under the control of Macchi, in the form of one of the latter company's MB 326 jet trainers on display.

come to accept that his family would have to cede 51 per cent of the Ducati equity to outside investors, whereas Gianfranco wanted to retain at least 51 per cent of control. Perhaps inevitably it was Claudio who eventually won the day, common sense prevailing over pride. In the 2 October 1996 issue of *Motor Cycle News* the final solution to these discussions was reported as follows:

> Ducati is set to double in size within four years, according to US investor the Texas Pacific Group, which has acquired a 51 per cent share in the firm in a £197 million deal. Former owner Cagiva retains a 49 per cent share. TPG partner David Bonderman said 'Ducati has a great product. We are enthusiastic to help it aggressively grow production and sales in the coming years'. Cagiva boss Claudio Castiglioni, who is chairman of the newly formed Ducati Motor SpA, said: 'Today marks a new era for Ducati.' TPG's other investments include a half share in Richard

Branson's Virgin Cinema Group, plus interests in Mexico, Latin America and China.

The official story behind the *MCN* headlines was that on 30 September 1996 Ducati had gained a new corporate structure, as Ducati Motor SpA. The Texas Pacific Group was one of America's leading investment funds, with headquarters in California and in Texas, headed by David Bonderman, founding partner James G. Coulter and William S. Price.

Besides Claudio Castiglioni as chairman of the new Ducati Motor, other senior posts were filled by Federico Minolti (chief executive officer), and Ing. Massimo Bordi, who was elected by the board as general manager, confirmation of the investors' faith in the Italian management.

The corporate restructuring programme drawn up by the new management team provided, for the immediate future, an investment of more than 70 billion lire, distributed

Massimo Parenti and Massimo Tamburini of the Cagiva Research Centre (CRC) were responsible for the styling, and items such as the forced air induction, on the ground-breaking Ducati 916 design.

over three years, which was intended to kick-start a recovery of production, which was at that time 120 motorcycles a day (for the reasons already related above, 1996 was to end with only 12,509 units sold). The broad intention was to increase this figure by at least 5,000 units a year, in order to reach a ceiling of 40,000 bikes produced in 1999.

This restructuring plan also provided for a growth in personnel, which was up by 180 people from the beginning of 1997, ending that year with a total staff figure of 750 employees.

For the financial year ended 31 December 1997, the new company generated gross sales of 386.3 billion lire. This represented an increase of 86 per cent over revenues of 207.2 billion lire in 1996.

In September 1996 Deutsche Morgan Grenfell Development Capital Italy was formed. Based in Luxembourg, this 135 million US dollar leveraged buyout fund began

A little-known fact is that the Cagiva factory in Varese was brought into the 916 production programme to cope with the demand. This photograph was taken at the Varese plant in December 1994.

taking majority positions in Italian companies, with Dante Razzano as its chief executive. This is of importance to the Ducati story because on 31 July 1998 at the Texas Pacific Group headquarters in Fort Worth, Texas, TPG, Deutsche Morgan Grenfell (DMG), Development Capital Italy and their co-investors announced that they had purchased the remaining 49 per cent of Ducati Motor SpA from Claudio and Gianfranco Castiglioni.

In a brief statement, Texas Pacific and DMG said: 'We were eager to invest more heavily in Ducati and the Castiglionis have wanted to pursue other business ventures. The agreement we reached benefits all concerned and it reiterates our satisfaction with the company's performance and prospects.'

And although no terms were disclosed it is my view, based on the initial purchase price of £197 million for the original 51 per cent back in 1996, that the remaining 49 per cent would have realized a total sufficient to give the Castiglionis something approaching £400 million. Taking into consideration the fact

(Above) *Abel Halpern of the Texas Pacific Group (left) with Ducati's design chief, Ing. Massimo Bordi. TPG purchased a majority shareholding in Ducati during September 1996, before a total buy-out from Cagiva in July 1998.*

Federico Minolti, Ducati's current managing director pictured in November 1997. The motorcycle is a 1998 model year 748BP (Biposto).

119

that Cagiva had purchased Ducati for almost nothing in 1985 this would seem a fantastic return. However, to give them credit, the Castiglionis had not only saved Ducati, putting the company back in contention, but had also invested significant amounts in the development of a string of new models (Paso series, Indiana series, SS series, Monster series, not to mention of course all the motorcycles that are the subject of this book – the four-valves-per-cylinder superbikes from the 851 through to the 916).

Even allowing for the debt mountain they had accrued during the early 1990s the Castiglionis came out of the Ducati sale with enough capital to relaunch themselves. Today not only are Cagiva and Husqvarna on the way back, with considerable invest-

Cagiva launched the long-awaited MV Agusta four-cylinder F4 in 1998. Designed by Massimo Tamburini (who has remained with Cagiva), will this glamorous machine prove a major threat to Ducati?

ment in parts back-up and production, but the Castiglionis have another ace card up their sleeves – the absolutely stunning Ferrari-inspired MV Agusta F4. *And* they also have the influential Cagiva Research Centre and its leader Massimo Tamburini, who after all created many of the best Ducatis, including the mould-breaking 916. Yes, in my opinion the Castiglionis may well be the real victors in all this, but only time will provide the ultimate answers.

10   Technical Appraisal

This chapter sets out to show the reader the main technical components within the engine assembly of the 916 series engines, which also encompasses the 748 and 996 models. Much that is shown in this chapter is also relevant to the earlier 851 and 888 four-valvers. This is not intended as a replacement for a workshop manual or even a stripdown sequence; instead it shows the reader what lurks inside that most charismatic of all modern high-performance motorcycle power units; the liquid-cooled, dohc, 90-degree Desmo Ducati V-twin, with fuel injection and six-speed gearbox.

It is also vital to realize that this state-of-the-art technology, with its Weber-Marelli electronic fuel injection and ignition systems, requires a maintenance programme. This is likely to prove even more expensive if *not* carried out. It also demands expertise, and the correct factory tools and diagnostic equipment. The days of the back-street mechanic or home maintenance are, as with the modern car, largely a thing of the past. Even so, most owners still like to know what goes on even if they have to employ someone else to do the actual work.

The technical whiz-kids who made this chapter possible. From left to right: Mick Walker and Moto Cinelli's famous trio of Jeff Green (technical manager), Iain Rhodes (workshop manager) and Paul Graves (technician).

Generator types

Machines up to the end of the model year 1997 all used Ducati generators and Ducati regulator-rectifier. From the beginning of the 1998 model year this began to change.

The first move was to replace the trouble-prone Italian-made regulator-rectifier with a Japanese Shindengen assembly. However, the Ducati generator remained. This involved a two-wire (input, AC) regulator-rectifier. In addition this latter item was also made available for older machines to replace the original Ducati item (the fitment of this new regulator makes the original charge warning light obsolete).

For 1999 a complete switch was made to Japanese electrics, with the use of a Denso generator. This is of the three-wire variety and so a new three-wire (input, AC) Shindengen regulator-rectifier was introduced. The handlebar switchgear remains of Italian origin, being of CV manufacture. But it should be noted that the four-valve models use a different type (but still CEV) to the two-valve models (SS and Monster series).

Desmo, 4-valve-per-cylinder, 90-degree V-twin Ducati engine, with oil cooler and Weber-Marelli integrated electronic fuel injection and ignition systems.

The bare right-hand (offside) crankcase (1996 and later) ...

... and its matching left-hand (nearside) half.

The close-ratio (916 SPS and Corsa) gear cluster mounted in the left-hand (near-) side. Again, the cases shown are those used from 1996 onwards; these supersede the previous type when ordered as replacement parts for pre-1996 machines. This includes two-valve Monster and Supersport models.

A bare left-hand case. This is pre-1996; note the castings for the kickstart boss as used on the Cagiva Dakar Elefant off-road racer, and the single 6mm bolt hole behind the starter motor. Later cases use two 6mm bolts and feature a revised oil baffle along the bottom of the case.

Matching right-hand case from a pre-1996 model.

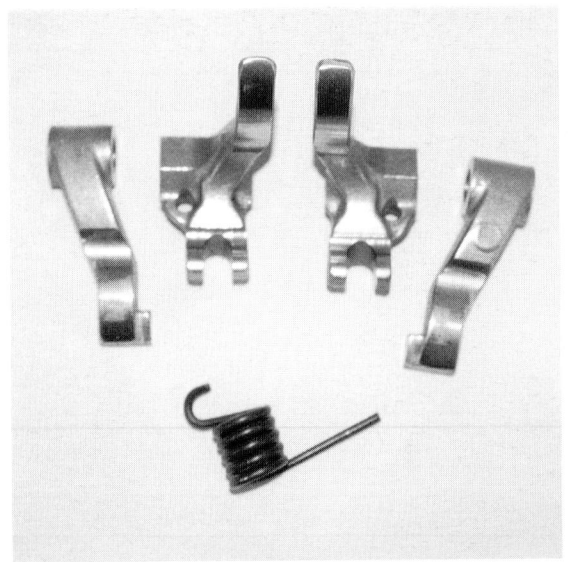

Two opening rockers (outer), two closing rockers (centre) and one anti-rattle spring (should be one per closing rocker).

Four-valve Ducati camshaft.

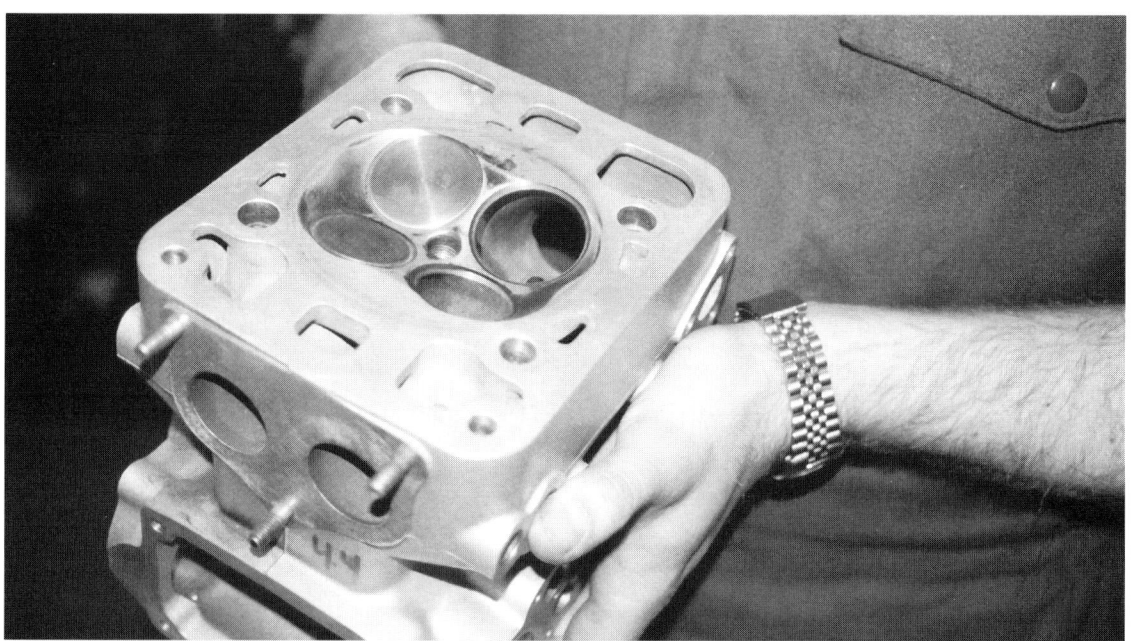

(Top) *Four-valve (SP) cylinder head. The same casting can be used for both front or rear cylinder fitment.*

(Bottom) *Side view of the cylinder head.*

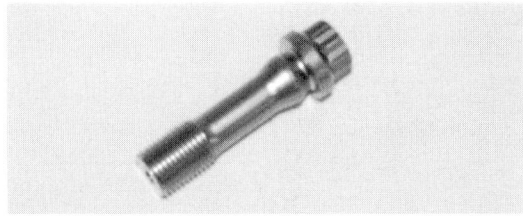

Big-end bolt (SP type).

(Above) *Crossover shaft. This transmits drive from the crankshaft to the cam pulleys.*

(Below) *Cylinder head oil feed pipe.*

Pair of primary drive gears. These are only supplied as a matched pair.

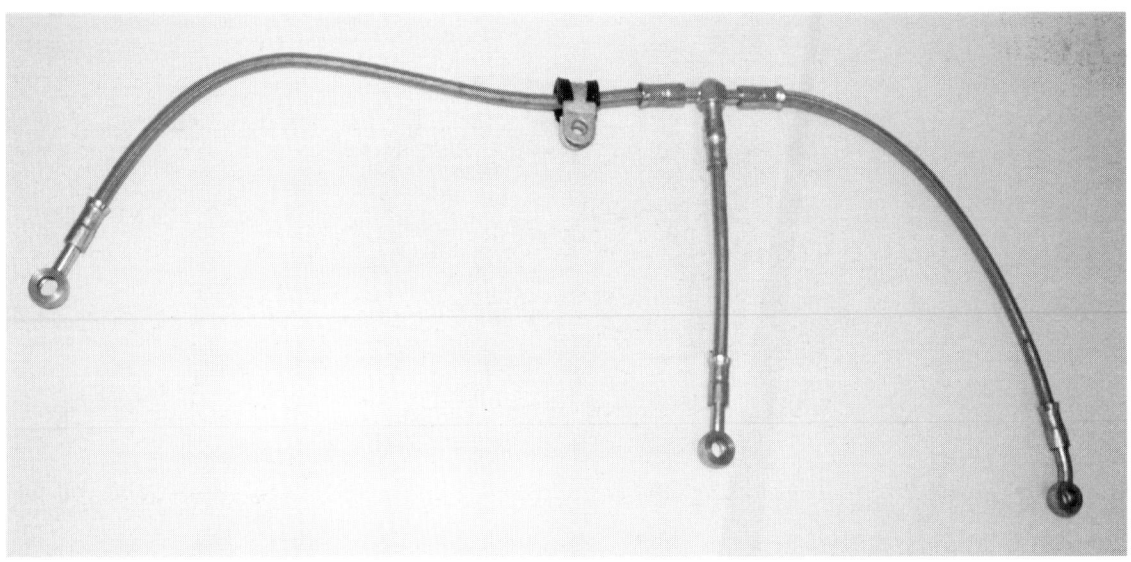

First / fourth and second / third gear selector forks and shafts.

(Below) *Crossover shaft gear.*

(Below right) *Clutch-hub drive flange.*

(Bottom) *Flywheel inner.*

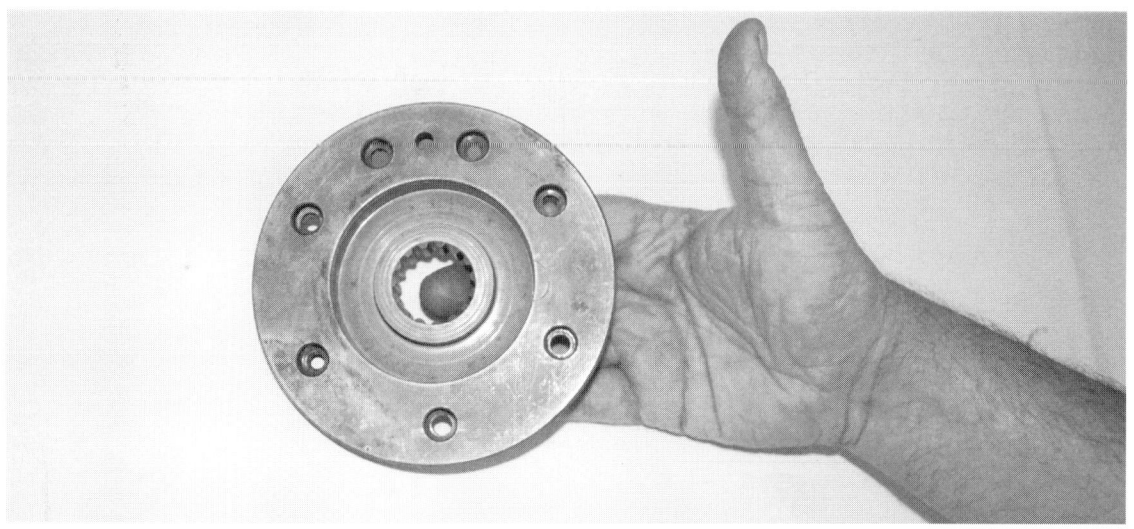

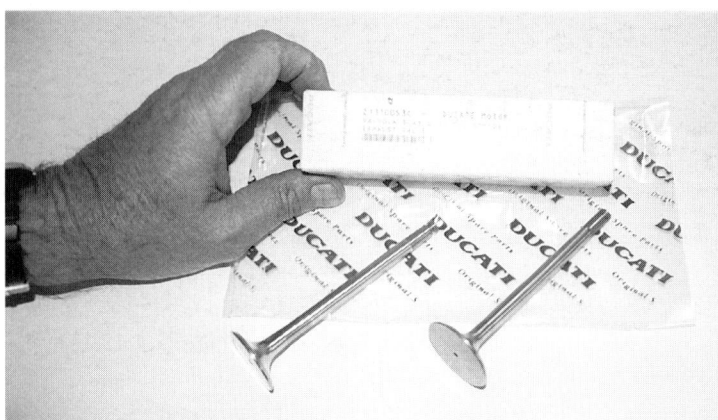

(Above left) *Starter gear and one-way sprag clutch bearing.*

(Above) *Starter gear, bearing race and shim.*

(Left) *SP inlet and exhaust valves.*

(Below left) *1994 Corsa (racing) gear linkage. Note the holes drilled in the arm and the alloy back.*

(Below) *Clutch housing items.*

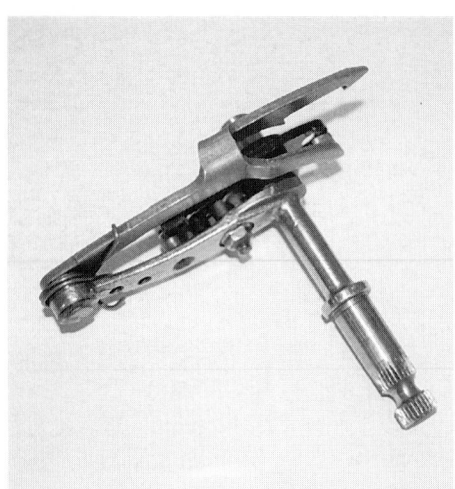

Starter idler gear.

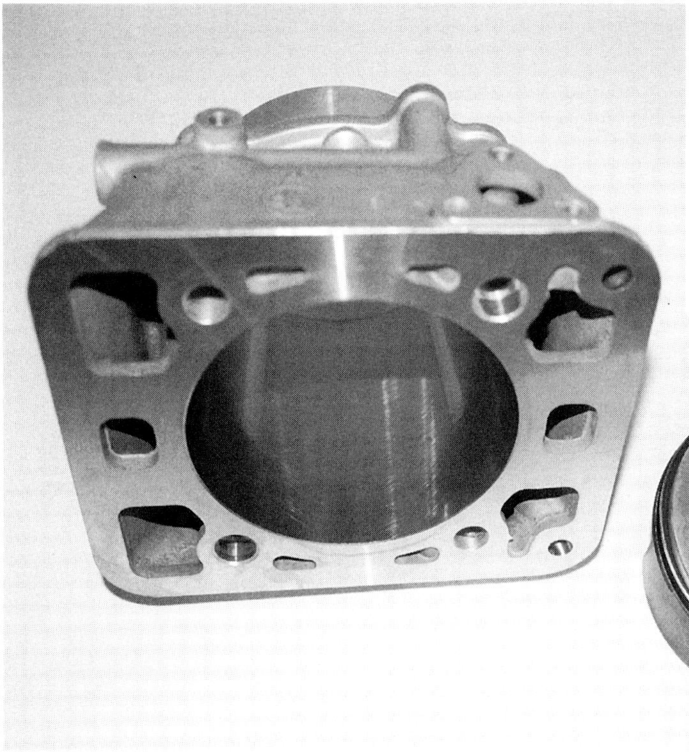

916 cylinder barrel and piston.

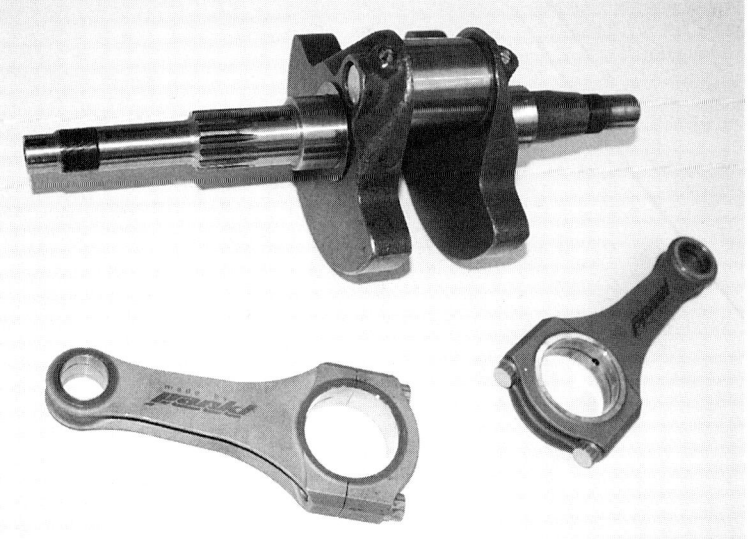

Crankshaft and SP con-rods. These are the Austrian-made Pankl steel connecting rods of the type used up to 1997. For 1998 Pankl produced titanium items. Both types are of racing quality, whereas many of Ducati's four-valve street models from 1989 use rods with a lower maximum rpm limit (see note at end of chapter).

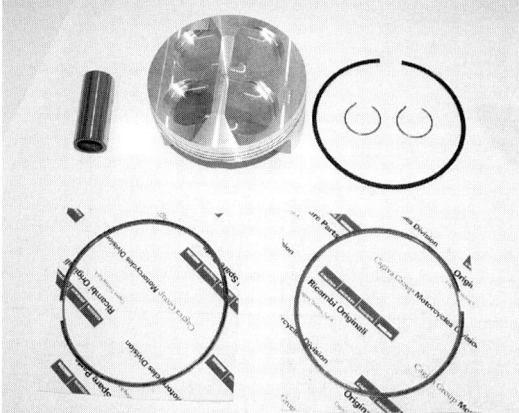

(Above left) *916 Biposto piston and higher compression Corsa racing item. All modern Ducati V-twins use forged pistons, except the 600 SS two-valver, which is cast.*

(Above) *Corsa piston with rings, gudgeon pin and circlips.*

(Left) *Generator cover and water pump assembly (Ducati-type generator).*

(Below) *916 Biposto oil pump. The SP version has the oil pressure relief valve built into the pump cover.*

(Right) *916 Biposto connecting rods. These are recommended for road use only.*

(Below) *Four types of connecting rod used in the 4-valve engine series. The latest racing rod is on the far left.*

(Bottom left) *Clutch-driven (plain) and driving (friction) plates, plus cush drive rubbers.*

(Bottom right) *Clutch case and cover plus clutch plate set.*

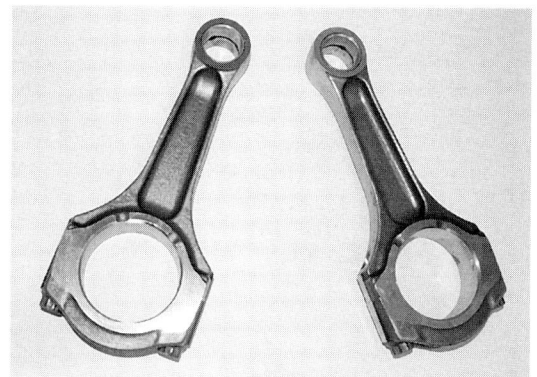

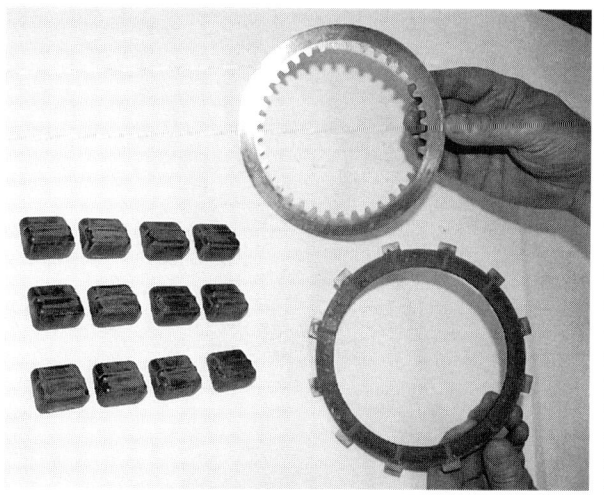

SP outer flywheel and cross-shaft gear. This photograph shows the different triggers used on the Biposto (see picture on page 127). The Biposto fuel injection system uses the gear teeth and a trigger in the form of a machined recess in the gear teeth to establish engine speed and position. This requires the use of only one pickup. The SP uses an older system that requires two pickups, one measuring engine speed from the outer flywheel and the other pickup sensing the engine position from the crossover shaft gear (note the triggers). The reason for this is that the SP runs four independent injectors (two per cylinder) like on the race machines, whereas the Biposto only has two injectors (one per cylinder).

(Left) Starter motor.

(Below left) Ducati stator and rotor. This assembly has been replaced by a Japanese Denso three-phase item for the 1999 model year.

(Below) Left: Corsa alloy selector drum (1994). Right: standard Biposto steel item, showing selector detent. This latter component was introduced with the 916 range and is now standard on all models.

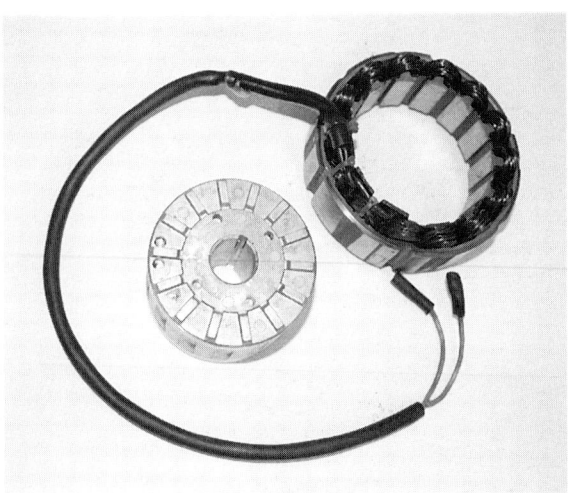

Single injector throttle bodies and IAW 1.6 M ECU fitted to the 916 Biposto. This is the system that uses the single engine pickup.

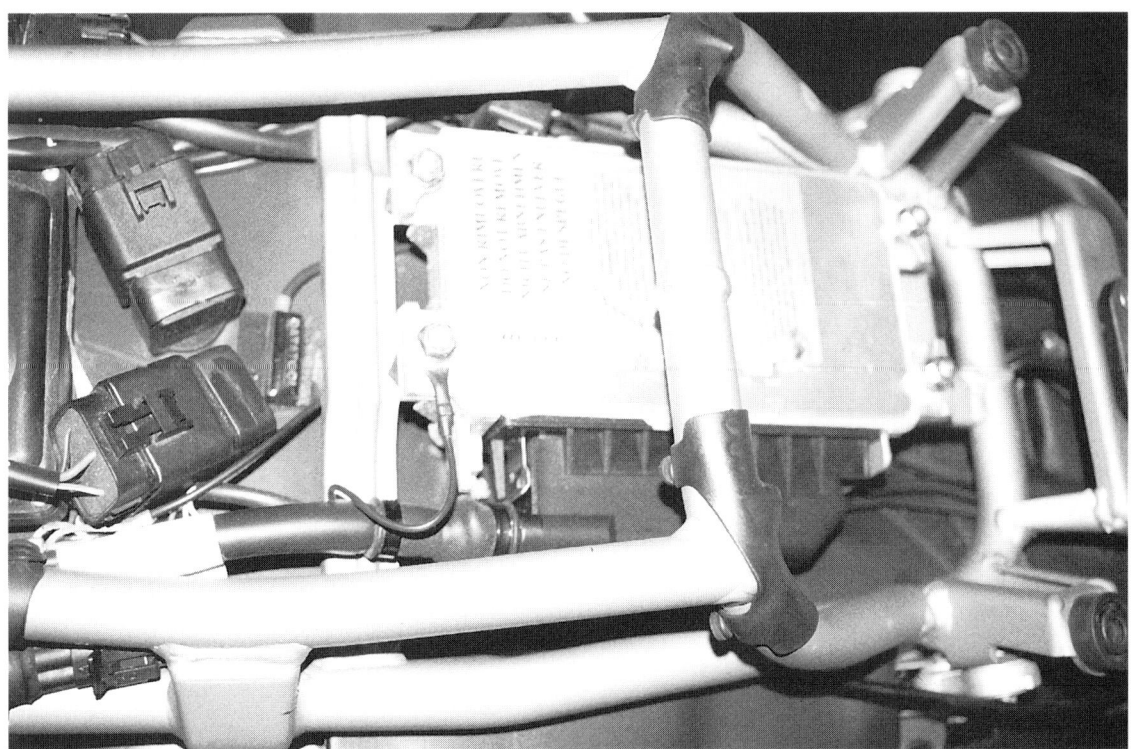

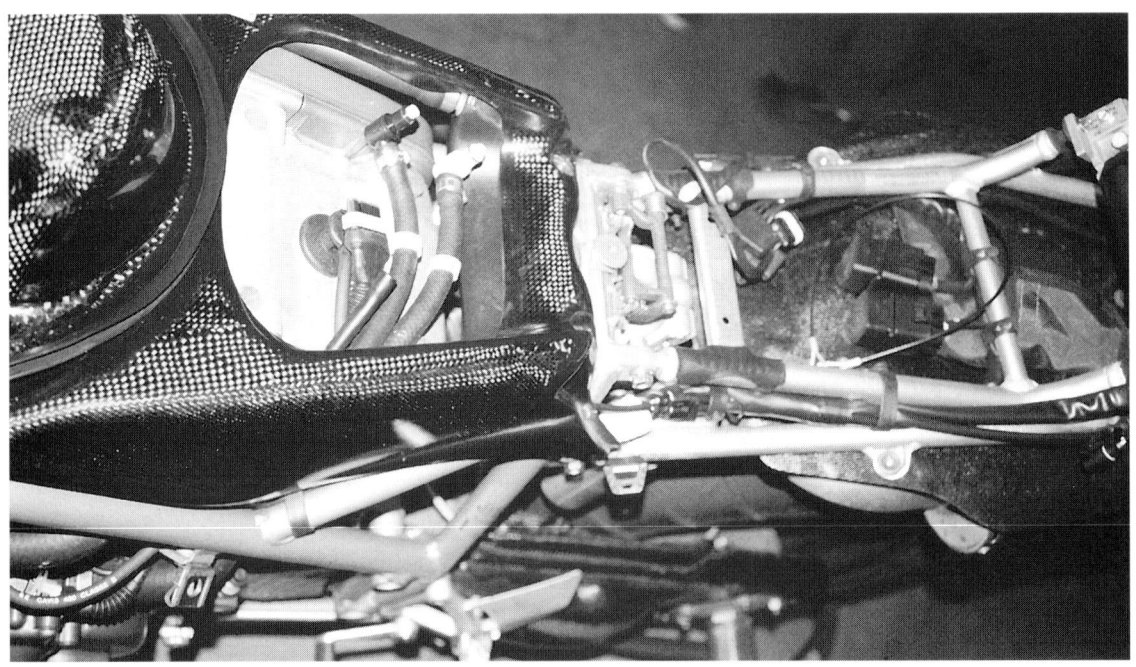

(Above) *Quick-release fuel lines are standard on all 916/748/996 models. The carbon airbox is from the Foggy Replica.*

Temperature sensors for fan, gauge and ECU – standard on all 916/748/996 models.

This photograph shows position of the second engine pickup (rev sensor) on SP/SPS models (mounted just below the rear coolant hose, above sight glass). Note that the 748 SP/SPS use the Biposto injection system as it does not require extra fuel.

(Below) *916 Biposto generator cover. Note the casting for the SP pickup is not machined.*

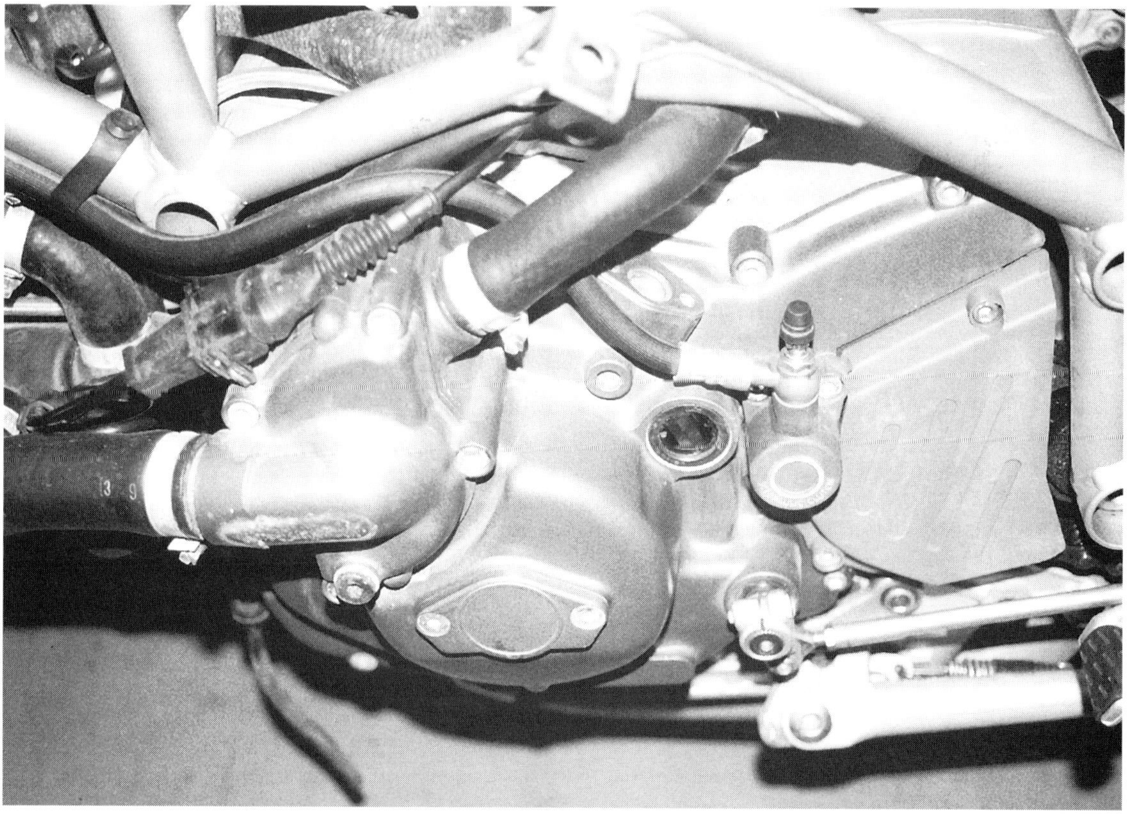

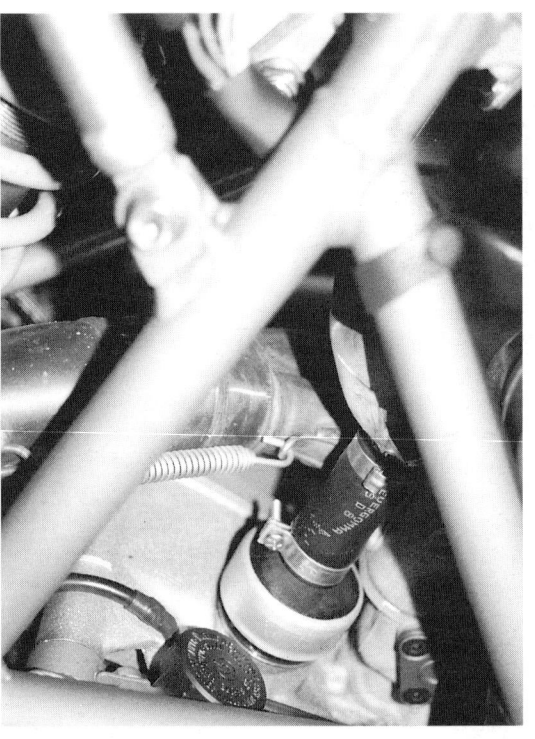

Eccentric chain adjuster clamp bolts at the rear of the swinging arm. This is standard on all 916/748/996 series machines.

(Right) Engine breather fitted to the top of the crankcase (revised for 1999 model year).

The large P8-type ECU (right) fitted to 916 SP/SPS models; also fuel pump, ECU relays and standard Ducati-supplied tool kit.

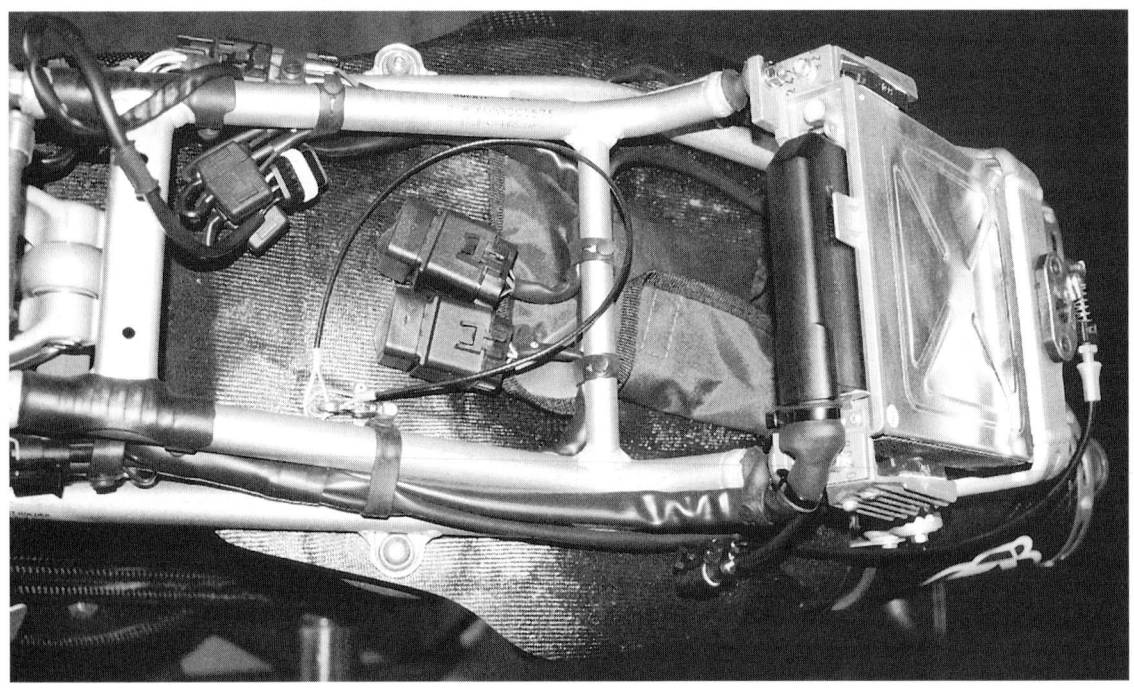

(Above) *CDI ignition module fitted to the sides of the ECU (SP/SPS 916). These items are built into the Biposto ECU unit. Note the Termignoni carbon-fibre silencers.*

Radiator, throttle body and electrical block connector – front right (offside) of engine.

(Opposite, top) *Twin injector throttle bodies as used on all 916 SP/SPS machines.*

(Opposite, bottom) *Radiator, fan, temperature sensors and so on – front left (nearside) of engine.*

(Right) *Oil sight glass and exposed clutch (916). Note clutch springs removed!*

Shindengen regulator. This component supersedes the old unit and is now standard fitment (from 1998 onwards) on all models. (See box on page 122 for additional details.)

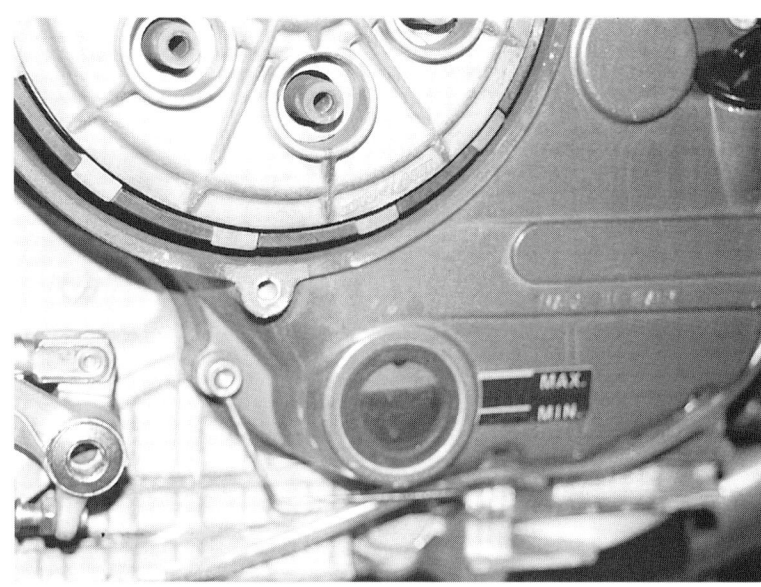

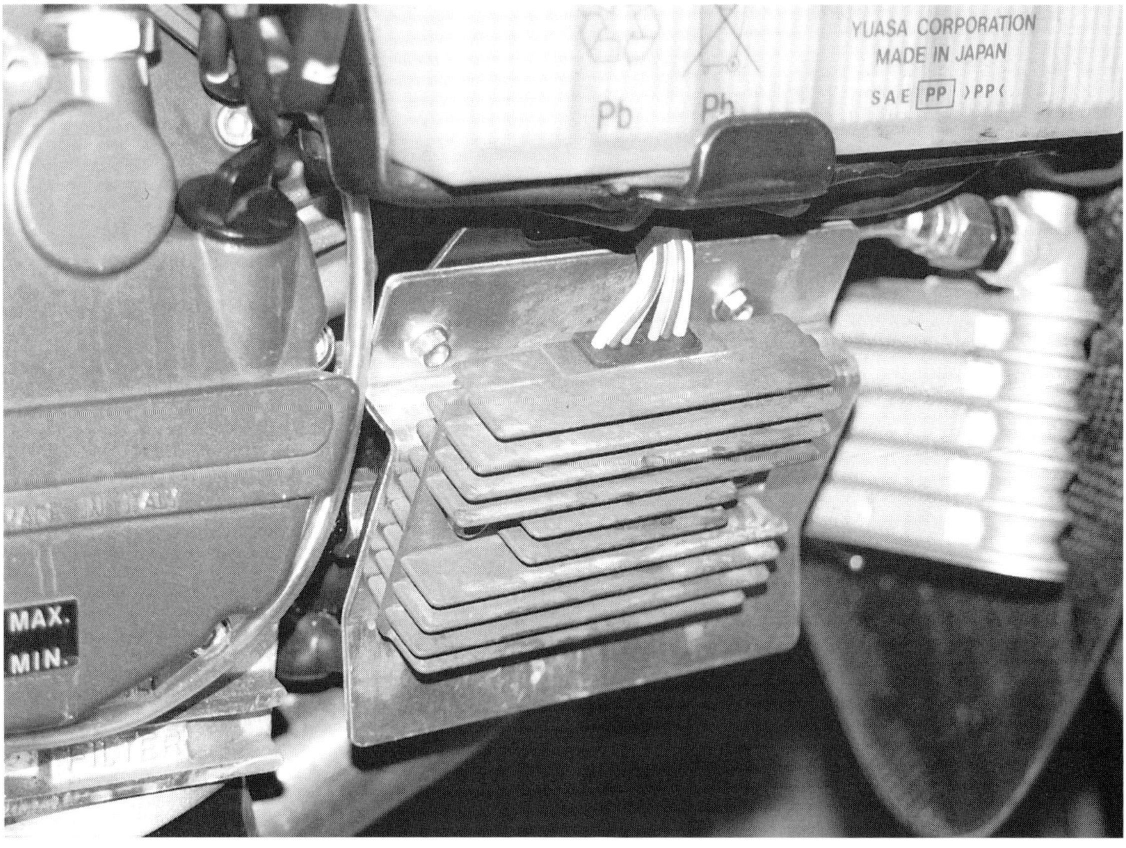

A Ducati dealer's tool board. All official dealers have them as a requirement for obtaining the franchise.

Mathesis tester. This diagnostic and set-up equipment is used on all injected Ducatis, and again is compulsory issue to authorized dealers.

140

11   The 996

First Ducati used their full 1-litre 996cc (98 × 66mm) engine in their World Super Bike factory racers. Next came the specialized and hyper-expensive SPS at almost £20,000 in 1997 (even though it was badged as the 916 SPS). But the really good news for all those *Ducatisti* who could neither afford the big bucks SPS nor be good enough for a

Looking for all the world like a standard 916 BP, the 996 offers even more performance. In particular, the increase in engine size has provided enough extra torque to surprise even hardened testers.

WSB factory ride came in August 1998, with the announcement that the 996cc 'big-bore' engine was to be made available in the much cheaper, but still highly desirable, BP (Biposto) model for only £11,400.

With this announcement the Bologna factory effectively signalled the end of the road for one of the world's most famous bikes, the legendary 916. As charted in Chapter 6, the 916 was publicly launched at the Milan Show in November 1993, although stock did not actually reach dealers until late spring the following year. It began an instant success story. There was a massive demand for the bike, which the factory could not match,

The 996 logo – small, but it means a lot!

Factory studio shot of the new for 1999 996; this is the Biposto (dual seat) version. Colour options are red or yellow.

Another 996 BP, this time being put through its paces in a race-track environment; this is one of the first of the new model to leave the factory.

leading to long (and hugely embarrassing) waiting lists.

The 916 simply changed the face of sports bikes in a way that only the original GSX-R750 Suzuki had achieved a decade before in the mid 1980s. Almost five years on, the 996 BP is an improvement in terms of both power and engine torque, but still relies on the 916's running gear to a large extent. It is very difficult to tell the two models apart. In fact the changes, while subtle rather than major, did amount to real improvements. These include those shown on the right.

In fact Ducati had answered the bulk of criticism made about certain aspects of the 916. The engine of the SPS had in fact been detuned for the new 996BP – but it was still to prove one of 'the hottest bikes on the road' (*Motor Cycle News*, 9 September 1998). Indeed, for anyone waiting to upgrade their existing 916 BP to something more exciting the 996 BP was the ideal choice.

The engine of the 996 BP has twin fuel injectors, against the 916 BP's single injector

> Revised engine with 4mm bigger pistons; the bore, at 66mm, remained unchanged
> Primary drive gearing altered to provide more bottom end drive
> The braking system from the 916 SPS, with new, thicker 5mm steel discs and PSC16 master cylinder (the same as the two-valve 1998-type 900 SS)
> Larger silencers to meet 80dB noise limits
> New PSC13 clutch master cylinder
> Redesigned seat fitting for more security
> Ducati logos on tank and 996 logo on fairing panel. Even this last section was a positive move, as many buyers of the 1998 Ducati four-valve models had complained of the lack of tank decals.

per cylinder. Power output is 113.5bhp against the 916 BP's 106bhp. The race-bred SPS makes 124bhp.

To the casual (or even serious) observer it's very hard to tell the 916 and 996 BP apart. But it's a different story once you hop aboard

1999 Ducati 996 Biposto road test by Rod Woolnough

This is *the* bike to be on in 1999. It's the boss. Seriously good looking, like its immediate predecessors, but bigger, not to be messed with, commanding respect, but more relaxed in attitude.

The 996 initially felt taller than the 916, much taller than the 748. Funny, but it seemed to be a much bigger bike, although the specifications probably say that it is more or less the same size. Parked alongside a friend's Guzzi 1100 Sport, a bike which dwarfed the 748 Ducati, the 996 looked just as big. Hard to explain. A bike with serious presence. I suspect that the seat is raised just a bit higher to make room for the bulkier silencers tucked underneath but I can't think why else it should look so much bigger than previous incarnations.

The size of these cans is one of the most obvious differences in appearance between the old 916 and the new 996. The graphics have changed again too. The Ducati word is back on the tank, where it belongs, and the numerals 996 are written large on the fairing for all to see at a glance.

Upon riding the bike more differences become apparent. The brakes are improved, they feel more powerful and less inclined to deteriorate with repeated hard applications. Handling and steering feel 916-like. Peak power is similar to the 916 but the way the power is delivered is quite different. I was always aware of the seemingly endless power available on this bike. Loads of power, starting lower down the rev range than earlier 4-valve Ducatis, and delivery never gets really dramatic. It will pull from very low revs, 1,500 or so, without struggling and then just pulls harder and harder as the engine speed rises. By 6,000rpm it is really churning out some power and pulls hard up to 10,000 or more. The primary drive ratio is higher on this bike than on the 916 and I think that this reduces the

During the preparation of this book, my assistant Rod Woolnough rode many of the four-valve models over extended distances, including more than 2,000 miles on this 996 BP. He is seen here during his journeys, which took in much of Scotland in November 1998.

Nearside view of the Woolnough 996 test model. The lowlands of Scotland are the backdrop.

perception of drama on acceleration. Watch out though: the rear end of the vehicle which moments ago was half a mile ahead, approaches with tremendous rapidity! It is geared for 190mph, and the 996 will easily do 140 in fourth, with two gears to go.

At both high and low speeds, I found the riding position perfect for my 6ft frame; my tiny wife declared the pillion to be extremely comfortable. The 996 was very easy to ride anywhere: relaxed and fast on the simple bits, begging to be laid on it's side through the curves, always feeling capable and unflustered, always looking after its rider and passenger, always leaving them feeling that they could have gone a bit quicker, had they wanted to, and good in town too. There isn't a lot of steering lock but that wasn't really a problem. The suspension on the test bike was set up more compliantly than on any other Ducati HyperSports bikes I have ridden. It was probably on its standard settings and the result was that it floated over road bumps in a smooth and civilized fashion but still retained its ability to steer quickly and corner better than almost anything else on the road. (I'm still not sure here about the relative merits of the 748 and 996. Which one is the better road bike? One of them is the best bike ever, but which one?)

The 996 is The Boss. It exudes power, beauty, and an ability to outperform; it is the bike to be on at the end of the Millennium. I need one!

SPS

When Ducati launched the SPS version of the 916 for the 1997 model year its main purpose was for homologation SBK/FIM Sport Production events. This explains why it was still marketed as a 916, when in fact it was equipped with the larger World Super Bike-derived 996cc (98 × 66mm) engine displacement. This also explains why Ducati did not go for another colour scheme instead of the standard 916 red.

But as with the other SP/SPS models, the majority of the machines ended up with collectors and enthusiasts. In 1997 the reason road riders wanted to own an SPS was its larger engine size, which was at that time unique on a Ducati except one in pure racing form.

At a cost of at least a third more than the standard 916 BP, the first batch of SPSs (around 200) soon went. However, after that things changed when half-way through 1998 the Foggy Replica was announced. This not only upped the game, but brought with it something of a backlash, not only from existing SPS owners, who had thought they already owned the ultimate Ducati that could be used on the street, but also from fans asking why the SPS was not made to look far more different from the stock 916 BP; why not at least give it a different colour? In this latter respect the cheaper, less well-specified 916 Senna was far more likely to turn heads. The fact that the SPS does not look significantly different from other 916, 748 and of course now, 996 models in the Ducati range is bad news if you are buying one for prestige or pose value.

In a combined road test of the 916SPS and Bimota's 1,002cc four-cylinder, Yamaha-powered YB11 in the 18 March 1998 issue of *Motor Cycle News* this was pointed out in no uncertain terms, when a couple of SPS owners were interviewed:

> John Hollis, 32, a video and TV special effects artist and 916 SPS owner said: 'When I got my 916 SPS in March '97 I seemed to be the only one with one. Now there's a 916 on every corner. I might get an MV Agusta or Aprilia RSV1000 instead.' Estate agent Carl Bridgewater, 37, has sold his SPS. He said: 'I really want something really different. I guess I'm a poser at heart. I might go for a Bimota YB11.'

In March 1998 there were five (officially imported) lookalike bikes in Ducati UK's range: the 748 Biposto at £9,500; the 748 SPS at £12,250; the 916 Biposto at £11,400; the 916 Senna at £16,150 and the 916 (but of course 996cc) SPS at £18,650.

Besides its larger engine the SPS also benefited from cast iron brake discs, braided clutch and brake pipes, a front headlamp with dual parking light and wiring; modified final drive ratio, improved half handlebar fixing; performance muffler kit (together with performance chip), additional carbon-fibre bits and silver plate on top of the steering yoke for the individual series number of the particular bike.

General Specification 916 SPS (1997)

Displacement	996cc
Bore and stroke	98 × 66mm
Compression ratio	11.5:1
Max power (claimed)	136bhp @ 9,785rpm
Max torque (claimed)	71ft/lb @ 8,800rpm
Fuel injection	2 injectors per cylinder
Wheelbase	55.6in (1,410mm)
Seat height	30.8in (790mm)
Rake/trail	22.5–24.5°/ 3.6–3.8in (9.1–9.7cm)
Fuel tank capacity	18 litres (4imp. gal)
Dry weight	418lb (190kg)
Maximum speed	174mph (280km/h)
Standing quarter mile	11sec/124.5mph (200.3km/h)

(Right) Rock star John Martyn admires the Moto Cinelli road test 996 BP, November 1998. John lives in the Scottish Borders.

One of the faster and more expensive 996 SPS models on the company's stand at the Munich Show, October 1998. Apart from a higher level of tune, the SPS now came with Marchesini five-spoke wheels plus the usual SPS uprated braking and load of carbon goodies. But for many it was still too similar to the much cheaper Biposto – in appearance, if not performance.

Aftermarket accessories

Alongside the world-wide growth of Ducati into a major sales force has come perhaps an even greater thriving 'cottage' industry of add-on goodies and tuning accessories for the various modern four- (and two-)valve V-twins.

No other bike marque except Harley-Davidson has anything like the same appetite from owners for spending vast sums making their bike special. By far the biggest sellers are the myriad of carbon-fibre components – everything from body panels to engine covers, through silencers (mufflers) and even the likes of instruments faces!

Typical of the 'cottage' industry that has grown up around the modern Ducati V-twins in the aftermarket accessory sector is the Italian company Febur. Items shown here include magnesium swinging arm and fork yokes, a titanium rear subframe, carbon-fibre goodies and even a single-sided swing arm for the two-valve Monster series.

Official factory Ducati accessories are marketed via Gio.Ca.Moto (International) under the Ducati Performance label. Ducati have a 50 per cent shareholding in the company. Ducati Performance is the 1999 entrant of both Carl Fogarty and Troy Corser in WSB.

The factory itself had previously largely stayed clear of this vast potential market – until the Texas Pacific buy-in of September 1996. Since then Ducati have followed the lead established by Harley-Davidson several years ago of aggressively marketing their own range of add-ons through their dealer network. It seems likely, with the Americans gaining full financial control of the company in 1998, that this trend will accelerate. The new owners will no doubt have investigated the Harley-Davidson operation and know this is a potentially huge dollar-earner, not just in the US, but in countries such as Japan, Australia, Germany, Great Britain and, yes, even Italy.

The tuning side is a much less easy market for the factory to exploit, and will probably always remain so. The reader should realize there are good and bad tuners. So before enlisting the help of one I strongly advise you to check out the tuner's competence if possible with previous customers who have already had work done. Don't be tempted to simply go for the 'sweet talk'. Unfortunately with the growth in Ducati's success some so-called specialists who are not quite as good as they purport to be have appeared. Finally, the best form of tuning is careful preparation, not radical alteration. This is because Ducati have spent vast amounts of money arriving at where they are today, so it is extremely difficult for anyone else to improve on this, except in the area of attention to detail (blueprinting).

Finally it is worth pointing out that Ducati's own accessory arm is Ducati Performance, run by Gio.Ca.Moto International on behalf of the Bologna factory. Gio. Ca.Moto and Ducati each have a 50 per cent shareholding, an arrangement which began at the end of 1997. Ducati Performance ran the team which saw Carl Fogarty win the 1998 WSB (World Super Bike) racing title. And in 1999 Ducati Performance are the only official factory-backed squad, with two riders – Fogarty plus the Australian Troy Corser.

and take the larger-engined model for a spin. Almost instantly you realize it has not only got more power, but more torque too – and surprisingly seems smoother for good measure. No wonder the September 1998 *MCN* test ended by saying, 'If you've always lusted after a 916, think again – it's a 996 you want now'.

The 996 BP will pull strongly from 3,000rpm, and by 5,000 it is charging hard, something it continues to do with a linear power curve all the way up to the rev limiter (which is set 1,000 revs lower than the 916 BP, at 8,500rpm). In fact the power delivery is best described as lazy, but when you need to change a gear, the 'box is extremely slick. The *Motor Cycle News* tester was impressed, too, saying 'every shift has your arms straining at their sockets as the torque floods in at 8,000rpm. The pull is addictive and there's nothing else to do but grip hard with your knees as it pushes you back in the seat.'

Even though it has a pillion pad, the 996 BP is not really a serious two-up bike; certainly if you want a four-valve Duke for this purpose, go for the new ST4 (*see* Chapter 13). With its monster gobs of torque anyone brave enough to become a 996 BP passenger is guaranteed a white knuckle ride! If you have to have the 916/996 looks but need to take a pillion, my advice is to plump for the 748 BP or, best of all, the far more suitable ST4. But for solo use nothing in the Ducati range (except the Foggy Replica or SPS versions) can touch a 996 BP for all-round ability *and* style. Come to think of it, the same applies to the competition. The 996 BP is that good. Ducati are working on its replacement already. But with the 916's creator no longer with them, the new head of Ducati styling, Pierre Terblanche, has a tough act to follow – and one that could well spell trouble for the new American-owned Ducati company if he gets it wrong.

The Ducati Experience race school

The Ducati Experience refers to a race school run jointly by the Brands Hatch Leisure Group and British Ducati importers Moto Cinelli. Since its launch one February day in 1998, the school has proved itself one of the very best in Britain, probably in Europe. The first year of its operations saw a squad of 748/916 models ready for customers to sample, backed up by not only the best circuits (Brands Hatch, Cadwell Park and Oulton Park), but also a team of experienced instructors.

For 1999 the Ducati Experience introduced one-to-one tuition from some of the top British road racers including Matt Llewellyn, Steve Plater, Mark Philips and Shaun Brown.

The author took part in a special track day organized by Ducati Experience at Cadwell Park on Monday 15 March 1999. Having taken part in a day at Brands Hatch the previous year I was immediately able to see the benefit of the new one-to-one tuition, instead of the 1998 multi-rider/instructor set-up.

Before being let onto the track a briefing takes place, including things such as riding technique, trackcraft, flag signals, safety and how cones are arranged at peel-off points around the circuit. As

The author (seated on the machine) with instructor Shaun Brown. Shaun is typical of the school's instructors, having had a long racing career, in his case specializing in true road circuits, such as the Isle of Man TT mountain circuit.

only one rider goes out with an instructor it means there are less people out on the circuit at the same time. Race school customers have the choice of either using their own riding gear or having it provided. Whichever you opt for, the important issue is being comfortable on the motorcycle (748 normally, or 996 for more advanced pupils).

When your track time comes around you follow your instructor out onto the circuit. For the first part of the session you follow him, which after all is sensible. Later you will be pulled in, points discussed with him and then you resume your riding, but usually you in front of the instructor noting your progress (or otherwise).

My session (with Shaun Brown) lasted 40 minutes, which is quite a long time to be circulating a race circuit. It's an 'experience' which I would recommend to anyone, I really enjoyed it.

Most of the forty-nine school days are at Cadwell Park in 1999, forty to be precise; the rest are eight at Brands Hatch, and one at Oulton Park.

The author piloting one of the Ducati Experience race school machines (a 748 here, but 996s are also available for the Advanced Course); Cadwell Park, spring 1999.

12 Foggy Replica

The background to the Foggy Replica is best explained by Hoss Elm, managing director of Moto Cinelli, the British Ducati importers (here speaking in 1998):

> Following his sensational victory on a privately entered Ducati at Donington Park in the World Super Bike series in 1992, Carl Fogarty desperately wanted an official Ducati ride; and at the end of that season I started negotiations for his contract with the factory. Carl was finally signed in January 1993 to ride with Giancarlo Falappa in the Raymond Roche squad.
>
> My effort in signing Carl for the factory team paid off when they agreed to let Carl ride for Moto Cinelli in selected races in the UK during the 1993 season. This he did brilliantly on a Moto Cinelli 93 Corsa, winning both legs of the North West 200 in Ulster, breaking the lap record. A few weeks later he repeated the performance at

Costing a cool £20,500, the limited edition UK-market-only 1998 Fogarty Replica is perhaps the ultimate factory-built collector's motorcycle.

The 1998 916 SPS Fogarty Replica Limited Edition

Engine	V-twin
Valve system	4V desmodromic
Displacement (cc)	996
Bore and stroke	98 × 66mm
Compression ratio	11.5:1
Max. power	123bhp @ 9,500rpm
Max. torque	10.1lb/ft @ 7,000rpm
Cooling system	Liquid
Fuel system	Electronic injection
Gearbox	6-speed
Length × width × height	80 × 30 × 42.5in (2,030 × 780 × 1,080mm)
Wheelbase	55½in (1,410mm)
Seat height	31in (790mm)
Fuel tank capacity	17 litres (3.75imp. gal.)
Front suspension	Inverted forks 43mm with compression, rebound and pre-load adjustment. Travel 127mm
Rear suspension	Progressive linkage monoshock with compression, rebound and pre-load adjustment. Travel 130mm
Front brake discs	2 floating rotors 320mm diameter
Rear brake discs	220mm diameter
Front tyre size	120/70 ZR 17in
Rear tyre size	190/50 ZR 17in

Features

- Carbon-fibre front fender
- Carbon-fibre underseat heat protection
- Carbon-fibre airbox
- Carbon-fibre rear mudguard/number-plate holder
- Öhlins steering damper
- Öhlins rear shock absorber
- Titanium con-rods
- Lightweight frame in $25CrMo_4$ steel
- Cast iron floating front disc brakes

Donington Park in the British Supercup series, scoring two wins and the lap record – a first for Ducati in both events.

Carl then joined the Virginio Ferrari team for 1994 and went on to make history and win the World Super Bike title in 1994 and '95.

I have always remained in close contact with Carl and considered his link with the factory to be vital to Ducati's success in the UK. Certainly Moto Cinelli's advertising campaign in 1997, which featured Carl and his family, proved to be the most popular in our history and helped us to achieve record sales.

When discussing the 1998 contract for Carl with the factory, I had the idea of a replica. In the following months I agreed the final specification with Ducati. The total build quantity of 200 [202 actually]

The man himself, Carl Fogarty – truly a legend in his own lifetime. Yet the 'Blackburn Bullet' is much more at home with his wife and family than in the media spotlight.

units will ensure that the model is one of the most exclusive ever produced in Bologna.

I feel that we have produced a fabulous machine that is a fitting tribute to one of Britain's greatest ever motorcycle racers.

With only 202 examples built (all in 1998), the 916 SPS (actually 996cc) Fogarty Replica is a limited edition that is virtually guaranteed to rise in value more than any other 916/748 series model. I was lucky enough to ride one of the very first examples on an extended test during August 1998. And of all the motorcycles I've been fortunate enough to test down through the years from all around the world, the 'Foggy Rep' has to rate as one of the top handful of true classics.

My first impression – and a lasting one – is of the truly awesome linear power delivery; a seemingly flat power curve that allows the rider to tap instantly into the power curve. This is unlike many modern machines, which only give of their best in the upper regions of the rev range.

Of course the basics are those of the less glamorous, but still heady, 916/748 series. But the Foggy Replica scored on its extra abilities in terms of power, suspension and braking performances. You feel that you can do almost anything. Of course, all this is fine in the controlled environment of a race circuit, but what about out on the ordinary highway? There's no need to worry – this is a bike that is incredibly easy to ride despite its scintillating performance. That word performance again, I hear you say, but with the 996cc (although officially labelled as a 916!) there is a claimed 123bhp at 9,500rpm (at the crankshaft).

Based on the 1998 916 SPS the Fogarty Replica has the following additional equipment:

Carbon-fibre seat unit
Five-spoke aluminium alloy Marchesini wheels painted black, similar in design to the 1998 race bike
Titanium/carbon fibre exhaust silencers with EPROM to suit (additional to standard items fitted)
Tecnosel seat (additional to standard seat unit fitted)
Carbon-fibre swinging arm protector
Colour-matched mirror bodies (red)
Racing-type paddock stand
Model-specific user guide
Special key holder
Specific model cloth cover
Certificate of authenticity
Model-specific production number-plate

Fairing panel removed to show the right offside view of the Foggy Replica's engine. Note also the dry clutch, battery location, radiator and oil cooler.

(Right) *From the left side (nearside) it is possible to see the sprocket cover, gearchange, prop stand, rear shock, water pump hosing and exhaust header pipes from the front and rear cylinders.*

The overall look of the Fogarty Replica mirrors the 1998 works racing machines with red paintwork and white 'race number' sections on the tailpiece and fairing frontal cowling. 'Ducati Performance' graphics (in white) are to be found on the sides of the lower fairing and the sides of the fuel tank. There are Moto Cinelli logos in white on the fuel tank and the upper part of the seat tailpiece between the race number areas. A Carl Fogarty signature graphic is located on the top section of the fuel tank, with the famous 'Foggy Eyes' on the windshield.

The above paintwork graphics are lacquered over as part of the overall finish of

The rider's eye view of the controls, switchgear, instrumentation and top yoke (triple clamp in the USA) plus Öhlins hydraulic steering damper. Note the individual number plate on the top yoke, denoting numbers one to 202 in the series.

(Below) *The famous 'Foggy Eyes' logo.*

(Below right) *Swedish-made Öhlins rear shock, the best there is.*

the machine. In addition, a sponsors' graphic kit was provided to the customer for fitment as required.

Unlike many other Ducati models, the Fogarty Replica was never sold as a 'grey import'. This is because it was a UK-only model; its £20,150 price (1998) being the usual price it was actually sold for. With only 202 examples manufactured in 1998 there was simply no need for dealers to offer discounts.

As with the famous Mike Hailwood-Replica bevel V-twin of two decades before, the Foggy Replica was a celebration of a racing legend, and the part Ducati had played in the success this particular rider had enjoyed.

The carbon-fibre 'chin' protector partly covers the oil cooler and front cylinder. Note the regulator mounted on an alloy plate to the rear of these.

(Below) A special feature of the Foggy Replica is the carbon-fibre swinging arm protector.

The black, five-spoke aluminium alloy Marchesini wheels are similar in design to those on factory race bikes.

(Below) *The front brake on the Foggy Replica. This shows the latest type of caliper introduced in 1997 on the ST2 and SP variants of the 748 and 916. The disc is a fully floating, cast iron component, again as found on SP and SPS versions.*

(Below right) *Hoss Elm, boss of British Ducati importers Moto Cinelli based in Northampton.*

As a footnote it is interesting to note that actually only 199 Foggy Replicas were released for general sale. The other three went to Hoss Elm (of British importers, Moto Cinelli), Carl Fogarty himself and to the factory's recently opened museum.

(Left) *Exclusive titanium / carbon-fibre exhaust silencers (with EPROM to suit) as specified for the Fogarty Replica.*

'Letter-box' light units (of CEV manufacture) are a feature of all 916, 748 and 996 models, including the Foggy Rep. Note the white number-plate background.

The inscribed and numbered key fob that came with each Fogarty Replica.

(Above) *Actual machine (number two in the series) presented by the factory to Carl Fogarty. It is pictured here at Moto Cinelli's Northampton headquarters in August 1998 before the handover.*

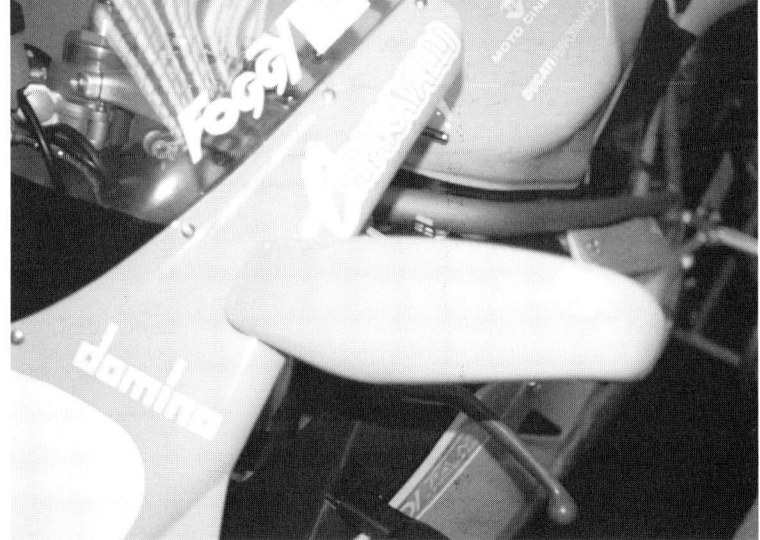

Colour-coded mirrors (red) and some of the decals on the Fogarty Replica. The logos are largely in white, with red relief.

Lionheart

Carl Fogarty is a rider who, more than anyone else, 'symbolizes' the World Super Bike Championship. His character and charisma are the maximum expression of the dynamism of this championship. For his legions of fans, he is simply 'King Carl', a legend. He is also the most successful rider ever in World Super Bike. His honours include three world titles with Ducati and forty-eight race victories, forty-four of which he has picked up on the twin-cylinder Italian machine.

His first World Super Bike race win came in 1992 on a Ducati 888 bought and financed by his family – a true privateer victory. From there it was on to the factory works team. When Super Bike racing hit the big time in 1994, Ducati and Carl Fogarty were ready. Worldwide television audiences saw a new phenomenon; the outrageous new Ducati 916, a bike so beautiful it became an icon of style beyond the boundaries of motorcycle sport. The pure aggression and will to win of the laser-eyed Englishman and the stunning performance of the 916 made for a combination that was impossible to beat for two years, a combination that set all the records in World Super Bike: most wins, most pole positions, most double wins, most fastest laps, most top-three finishes.

Ducati and Carl Fogarty have made motorcycling history together. Ducati stand as the epitome of daring Italian style, storied tradition, and the proposition that engineering can be art. The 916 could not have been designed and built in any other country. If you were casting around for someone to represent the mythical qualities of the English, the never-say-die spirit, someone as English as roast beef, you would pick Carl Fogarty, a man happiest at home with his family, away from cameras, interviews and publicity.

But this is also a man for whom coming second means being the first loser. His craving for victory is the quality that fans most appreciate all over the world. Certainly the Italian public has taken Carl to its heart. Anyone who can bring a red Italian bike (or car …) to the chequered flag first is a hero in Italy, but with Carl it goes further than that. To the Italian Ducati fans he is Lionheart. A very English name, but you will see it written on banners at Monza and Mugello – not just Donington Park and Brands Hatch.

In Japan you will see fans waving Union Jacks with Fogarty's name printed on them. In Spain, where Super Bike is less popular, Carl is the only well-known rider in the class, the Ducati man with the dancing eyes. In the USA, he plays a different role. There he is the guy in the black hat, the baddy, the gunslinger – and Carl enjoys that reputation perhaps as much as he does the English adulation back home.

Before Fogarty's first World Super Bike title in 1994, motorcycle racing hardly got a mention in the British media. Now Carl Fogarty is a household name, Britain's first truly famous motorcycle racer since Barry Sheene. But with the hero-worship comes pressure. Ever since he got to his feet in the sandpit at Donington Park's Maclean's Corner after a very short stand-in GP ride in 1990 and saw a sea of faces staring at him all registering total disappointment, Carl Fogarty has felt the pressure of his home fans' expectation heavily. He had not realized anybody cared, thinking he was just racing for himself. Perhaps now he even cares too much, and takes risks at home races just to fulfil fans' expectations.

The Fogarty Replica celebrates the guts and talent of a racer who has helped make the Ducati marque legendary, a man from Blackburn who conquered circuits and the hearts of fans around the world.

Date and place of birth	1 July 1966, Blackburn, Lancs	1992	Endurance World Champion 9th place, Super Bike World Championship	(Ducati)
First race	1983	1993	2nd place, Super Bike World Championship	(Ducati)
Career Achievements		1994	Super Bike World Champion	(Ducati)
1988	Formula 1 World Champion	1995	Super Bike World Champion	(Ducati)
1989	Formula 1 World Champion	1996	4th place, Super Bike World Championship	
1990	FIM World Cup Formula 1 Champion	1997	2nd place, Super Bike World Championship	(Ducati)
1991	7th place, Super Bike World Championship	1998	Super Bike World Champion	(Ducati)

13 The ST4

My first ride on the new ST4 came on a cold, wet and windy day in early January 1999. What a day to try out Ducati's latest, I thought. Especially since, of all the current Ducatis I'd tested over the previous twelve months, the model I liked least was the two-valve ST2 sports-tourer (albeit with panniers fitted and non-standard taller screen).

But it just goes to prove that you should never judge a book by its cover or, in this case, a bike by its appearance. Maybe because I was not expecting the ST4 to be my

Latest in the line of four-valve Ducatis is the new-for-1999 ST4 sports/touring model.

type of bike and because of the extremely bad weather conditions, the shock – for all the right reasons – when I rode the bike was truly immense. I have to say hand on heart that I instantly felt at home. Well wrapped up against the elements, I felt quite happy to contemplate one of my favourite rides – Wisbech to Scarborough, a distance of around 140 miles (225km) – which encompasses all sorts of countryside from the flatlands of South Lincolnshire to the hilly wolds near Cadwell Park, semi-motorway near the Humber Bridge and then into the dales of East Riding of Yorkshire and eventually the seaside resort of Scarborough. There are not very many machines with which I would have felt as confident about completing this trip in safety, comfort and enjoyment as I did with the unfamiliar ST4.

For anyone who lusts after a 916-style racer-for-the-road but cannot accept the narrow focus racing stance, or for someone who wants to carry a pillion, or of course for what Ducati designed the ST4 for in the first place, this really is the *ideal* bike. It is certainly my favourite modern Ducati if, as I do, I want to use the machine and carry a passenger and still retain the all-important 'grin factor', which the four-valve Ducati V-twin engenders.

It also handles surprisingly well, a point that *Motor Cycle News* made in their 23 December 1998 test: 'The chassis is taut so it can take full advantage of the legendary 916 engine. It has that typical Ducati 'steers-slow-turns-fast' feeling where you need a lot of steering effort to get the bike to turn.'

So why did Ducati feel they needed a more powerful brother for the two-valve ST2, which was introduced to the public at the Cologne Show back in September 1996? For starters, the ST2 has not only been well received by the press, but has also opened up a new customer base for Ducati. In its own press release for the 1999 model year

the factory's official handout contained the following:

Sport Touring

With the ST2, Ducati made its official début in the Sport Touring segment.

By entering this challenging market, Ducati designers and engineers took on a difficult task – to create a product that would satisfy the requirements of this category while at the same time remain faithful to the company's sport bike tradition.

In the period since its launch, the ST2 has received outstanding recognition in Ducati's key markets.

New for the 1999 model year, the ST4 redefines the Sport Touring segment. The development of the model was based on the following principles: to create a versatile motorcycle with excellent handling, equipped with an engine which provides the same level of performance as the best four-cylinder Sport Touring models.

The ST4's main challengers would appear to be the four-cylinder (V-formation) Japanese VFR800 Honda and the three-cylinder (across-the-frame) British Sprint ST Triumph. Instead of going for the 996cc engine-size Ducati (wisely in my opinion) opted for the smaller displacement 916cc (94 × 66mm) mill. Even so, in the December 1998 *Motor Cycle News* test, the Ducati ST4 proved the fastest, recording an electronically timed 160.9mph (258.9km/h), against the Honda's 155.6mph (250.4km/h) and the Triumph's 150.5mph (242.2km/h). However, the British bike has the best torque figures of 65.8ft/lb @ 5,167rpm, against the ST4's 62.2ft/lb @ 7,145rpm and the VFR's 56.4ft/lb @ 8,549rpm.

In a previous test (following the world launch in October 1998) *MCN* had criticized the ST4's rear suspension. However, as they admitted in their December test, this was

Available in a choice of Italian racing red, black, silver and metallic dark blue, the new ST4 offers a potent challenge to Honda's class benchmark VFR800 V-four.

due mainly to the test bike not being set up correctly. *MCN* described what they found:

> With more time available we set the sag – the amount of spring compression taken by the bike's weight – to 10mm without any-one on board and 30mm with a 10-and-a-half-stone rider. This is also a good way to find out if the spring is strong enough for your weight. If you set it to 10mm without the rider and then can't get a range of between 25 and 35mm with a rider on board, you'll need a different spring.

The rebound damping was bumped up by three-quarters to a turn and the compression half a turn from the stock setting. *MCN* went on to comment, 'Now the bike handles well on all types of surfaces and in certain conditions even has a slight edge over the Honda and Triumph as the set-up is stiffer'.

Perhaps the most important area for a sports-tourer is comfort and the ease with which the controls can be accessed. With the ST4 it feels 'right' the first time you climb aboard. The position of the 'bars and footrests is just about perfect.

But what really makes the ST4 such an excellent machine is the engine. The fuel injection has been reprogrammed to make it smoother and more torquey than on the original 916. On the road this is instantly recognizable in the way the ST4's engine pulls cleanly from as low as 2,500rpm. This is particularly useful for two-up work. Even so the bulk of the power lies nearer the top end of the scale, so it is possible to ride the ST4 both leisurely and in a sporting mode – something many modern machines are not capable of.

The ST4 (1999)

Engine	Liquid-cooled, dohc, 4-valves-per-cylinder, 90-degree V-twin, belt-driven overhead camshaft
Bore and stroke	94 × 66mm
Displacement	916cc
Compression ratio	11:1
Maximum power (at crank)	105.6bhp @ 9,000rpm
Lubrication	Forced feed gear pump, with oil cooler
Ignition	Electronic IAW type
Fuel system	Weber-Marelli electronic indirect type, one injector per cylinder
Primary drive	Straight cut gears
Final drive	Chain 520
Gearbox	6 speeds, straight cut gears
Frame	Lattice type, round steel tubing
Front suspension	Inverted telescopic fork with 43mm stanchions. Adjustments: pre-load, compression and rebound damping
Rear suspension	Progressive linkage with adjustable monoshock
Front brake	Twin 320mm Brembo brake discs, 4-piston calipers
Rear brake	Single 245mm disc, 2-piston caliper
Wheels	3-spoke, light alloy
Front tyre	120/70 17in
Rear tyre	170/60 17in
Valve sizes	Inlet 33mm, exhaust 29mm
Valve timing	Inlet opens 11 BTDC/closes 70 ABDC
	Exhaust opens 62 BBDC/closes 18 ATDC
Length	81.5in (2,070mm)
Width	36in (910mm)
Height	46.5in (1,180mm)
Seat height	32.3in (820mm)
Ground clearance	6½in (165mm)
Fuel tank capacity	21 litres (4.6imp. gal)
Dry weight	473lb (215kg)
Maximum speed	161mph (259km/h)

ST4 vs ST2

Bearing in mind the SPS saga (*see* Chapter 11), Ducati have, I feel, made a serious mistake in not giving the ST4 a visible difference from the cheaper two-valve ST2. At least the factory's marketing department should have given the models different colour schemes! Instead, it is not until you actually take a test ride that you will discover just how much better the ST4 is. I feel this is a real shame.

But things are not what they seem in the actual engineering side of the ST4 versus ST2 stakes. The ST4 may *look* like its two-valve brother, but in fact it is far more than simply a change of engine unit.

For starters the cylinder heads of the 916 engine had to be re-engineered to fit the ST2-based frame; when Ducati technicians first applied themselves to the ST4 they soon discovered that in standard form the 916's engine assembly was simply too long!

Not only was there not enough room for the correct airbox (rear cylinder), but the front cylinder extended too far forward and would have made contact with the front tyre under extreme braking. This excess length also meant that the engine would have been mounted too far forward in the frame. So how did they solve it for the production ST4?

Essentially, a complete redesign of both cylinder heads was required to ensure that the engine was both narrower and shorter. This not only cured the airbox and front wheel problems but also allowed the engineers to place the powerplant at a point that retained the ST2's 49/51 front/rear weight bias.

Although it may not be obvious, there is also a different fairing on the ST4 than on the ST2. This is not only because of the engine itself, but also because of the airbox design and its ducting and the inlet manifolds. This latter detail was necessary to make sure that the power output came up to expectation. The exhaust system was also swapped to optimize peak power and torque outputs. The long, thin air duct that sits

An advertisement for the ST4 from the top-selling British weekly, Motor Cycle News, *January 1999.*

1999 Ducati ST4 road test by Rod Woolnough

The ST4 is a fine motorcycle. Designed by Ducati as a 'Sports Touring' bike, and it is and it does! Ducati have basically taken their ST2, replaced the old 944cc 2-valve engine with a 916 4-valve and called it an ST4. In doing so they have transformed the machine. The extra power seems to tighten up the whole bike. The handling and performance of the ST4 are a considerable improvement on the ST2.

This is the best tourer that Ducati have ever built. It is comfortable for both rider and pillion, with lots of room on board. The relationship between seat, bars and footrests lets the rider sit fairly upright, aided by the fairing, which cuts through the air very effectively, protecting both rider and passenger from wind pressure and buffeting. (Ducati offer a higher screen for the ST2, so there is probably one for this model, in fact they may well share the same screens; don't get one. On the ST2, the higher screen completely ruined the aerodynamics and caused some very disconcerting effects.) Weather protection is not so good; the fairing is very slim and you will get wet in the rain. A useful grab rail is provided for the pillion passenger.

The mirrors are amongst the best ever fitted to a bike. They are wide set and flexibly mounted so that they would easily fold back should they hit anything, but they are completely vibration free and offer excellent rear view. The headlight is also one of the best: brilliant and long ranged. The instrumentation is first class, including a useful clock and an accurate and reliable LCD fuel gauge. I was a bit disappointed that the levers didn't have span adjusters on them. There are both side and centre stands fitted and they are both easy to use; Ducati thoughtfully provide a neat little folding handle to assist in lifting the bike onto its centre stand. The side stand is of an improved design – much better than other models' inferior devices.

The ST4 is quick. It has 916 power and it shows. It's nearly as fast as its HyperSports brother is: I had no trouble attaining an indicated 150mph on a nearly new example and I have heard of ST4s managing true speeds of over 160mph. It provides thrilling acceleration, which must be nearly as fast as the 916 Biposto. It easily lifts its front wheel, but shouldn't really catch anyone out. The brakes are excellent; the front powerful and progressive whilst the rear actually works! Handling is top grade. The ST4 seems to steer a bit quicker than the 916, perhaps because of the narrower section rear tyre, a 170/60ZR17 instead of the 180 or 190 fitted to the sportier bike. It feels tall, but nice and light on the move. The suspension was set up quite softly on the test bike and this made the cornering just a bit less precise than it could have been with firmer damping, but progress over bumpy stretches was very smooth indeed. Spring and damping rates are fully adjustable; so fine-tuning is no problem. There's plenty of ground clearance, though some really enthusiastic riding might just graze the centre stand. Fuel consumption went as low as 32mpg but did better than 40mpg on some runs. I travelled over 150 miles on one tank full, and there was still some fuel left; that seems a reasonably long range to me.

The least aspect of the ST4 is the styling. It's not to my taste. Having said that, though, its appearance did grow on me and when on the move the exhilarating performance was compensation enough for it's slightly less than racy looks.

For someone who doesn't want to be stretched out over a petrol tank, someone that prefers a slightly more relaxed ride, but wants the performance, the ST4 would be a very good alternative to a 916 (replaced itself by the 996). It's quite a bit cheaper too! For someone who wants a Ducati tourer, this is the best one they've ever made. It doesn't turn so many heads as a 748, 916 or a 996, but it surprises an awful lot of people with its extremely capable performance.

The 916cc four-valve engine and ST2-based chassis combine to provide an extremely capable sports-tourer.

(Below) *The engine's cylinder heads had to be totally re-engineered to provide a narrower, slimmer power unit for the ST4. This was needed not only for the fitment of a suitable sized airbox, but to reduce the overall engine length.*

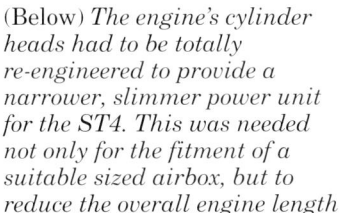

under the ST4 headlamp is there for a very good reason – to reduce noise. The engineering team needed to ensure that the ST4 was quieter both from exhaust and induction viewpoints.

One of the changes that is hard to spot is the vast improvement in rear brake performance over the ST2. This has been achieved by increasing the piston size from 32mm to 34mm. Owners and testers alike had criticized the ST2's braking as lacking in both power and feel. Obviously with the extra 26bhp of the ST4 four-valve engine a better rear brake was a necessity.

Yet another little known fact is that both wheels of the ST4 are lighter than those of the ST2 were when it was launched at the end of 1996. Using a new, aircraft aluminium some 3.1lb (1.4kg) has been saved. This means there is reduced centrifugal force, making the bike more manoeuvrable.

Both the front brake and clutch have improved remote master cylinders; these being coded PS16 and PS13 respectively. But unlike on the most sporting Ducatis, the levers themselves are non-adjustable.

Not only is the riding stance near perfect, but the ST4's instrumentation is user-friendly, with easy-to-read dials.

(Below left) *Don't assume that the ST4 simply makes use of the ST2's fairing, because although similar it is different.*

(Below) *Passengers are well catered for: not only does the ST4 have a comfortable dual seat, but a proper grab handle for extra security and piece of mind.*

The longer gear lever (from the Monster series) and superior side stand (but still of the instant flip-up type) are both improvements implemented as a direct result of complaints received from ST2 owners.

Ing. Massimo Bordi said at the ST4's launch in October 1998, 'We think we will sell more ST4s than ST2s, the ratio being as much as 70/30 in favour of the ST4.' Certainly I for one would much prefer to pay the extra (around £1,100 in Britain during early 1999).

Like with the ST2, Ducati produce a range of official accessories for the ST4, including hard panniers and two sizes of top box.

14　Future Developments

That Ducati can plan for the future is something of a miracle in itself, because if one studies the past it soon becomes clear that, besides making some of the most sought-after motorcycles on the planet, the company has also had something of a chequered history.

But survive it has, and that in itself is an achievement when so many other have not. A real turning point in the Bologna marque's history came in May 1985, when the Castiglioni family-owned Cagiva concern took over the reigns of power.

There is no doubt that Cagiva's involvement saved Ducati from extinction, certainly as regards motorcycle production. It might be easy to assume that the next owners, Texas Pacific Group (TPG), had done a lot – and so they had in the short time that they had been involved (from September 1996, the original 'buy-in' date) – but without the Castiglioni brothers there would have been no four-valve models and this book's story would not have been needed! In March 1999, Ducati was floated simultaneously on the stock markets in Milan and New York as a private limited company, but the influence TPG and its partners have made on the Ducati story is considerable.

Another of TPG's stated aims was greatly increased production. This could well pose another problem. Lots of Ducati's clientele like the idea of a product that is not only appealing, but is not to be seen on every

Ing. Massimo Bordi in pensive mood discussing the future.

street corner. Maybe Ducati are not Ferrari, but they could well learn from their Italian auto brothers in that Ferrari have a production limit of 3,000 cars per year. Will the Ducati customer base want to be more Ford than Ferrari? I doubt it very much.

Inauguration of Museo Ducati

In November 1998 Ducati Motor SpA proudly announced the official inauguration of Museo Ducati. Located within Ducati headquarters, the 1,000sq m museum highlights the fifty years of technological innovation, award-winning design and exceptional racetrack performance that have made the marque famous worldwide.

The permanent collection of twenty-six bikes recounts the rich history of the Bologna-based manufacturer, from the popular post-World War II 'Cucciolo' to the 996 – which recently won both the Riders' and Manufacturers' 1998 World Super Bike Championships.

Arranged on an illuminated racetrack, with a special multimedia theatre housed in a larger-than-life red crash helmet, the motorcycles can be admired up close in the museum's main hall. The adjacent six galleries are divided into specific 'families', ranging from the Cucciolo, Marianna and tri-camshaft racing twins to L-twin bevel gear engines, Pantah, and today's superbikes. Museo Ducati also displays a number of the company's earlier products such as radios, cameras and movie projectors, which made the Ducati brand synonymous with advanced technology in the first half of the century.

An NCR 900 bevel V-twin of the type used by Mike Hailwood during his dramatic winning comeback ride in the 1978 Isle of Man TT, on display in the newly created Ducati museum facilities.

Often displayed in museums around the world – including the Berlin Design Centre, the Museum Nazionale della Tecnica in Turin and most recently, the Guggenheim Museum in New York – Ducati motorcycles are as renowned for their unique Italian design as for their racetrack victories.

'*Ducatisti* will finally have a reference point where they can learn about the history and heritage of the company and its racetrack successes,' states museum curator Marco Montemaggi. 'Making this museum a reality has been an exciting endeavour, and it surely will be the fulfilment of a dream for many generations of *Ducatisti*.' Montemaggi's extensive research has revealed limited edition racing bikes, historic advertising campaigns, original racing leathers worn by legendary riders and numerous other Ducati artefacts. Original footage of both historic and recent Ducati races are projected on the various monitors in the museum.

With over twenty years of experience at Ducati, general manager Massimo Bordi notes this historic event. 'Walking around the museum moves me a great deal, as I recall moments of glory as well as more difficult times. But this museum surely represents a new era for Ducati.' Montemaggi explains the layout:

Divided into nine main sections, the museum reiterates the chronology of Ducati's evolution from small electrical company to motorcycling giant. Each section describes a major period in the company's technological development along with the key personalities that have made Ducati the leading light at racing circuits the world over.

The story begins in 1946 with the Cucciolo, Ducati's first engine. Up to this point, the company, which was founded in 1925 by the Ducati brothers, had mainly been concerned with electro-mechanical manufacturing. Then the Taglioni era begins with the arrival of the legendary engineer at the company, a man who became famous for, among other things, the desmodromic valve system. From Taglioni to the present day, desmodromic valve gear would distinguish Ducati bikes. The great Taglioni was also responsible for the very successful Mariana 100 and 125 Gran Sports, kings of the Moto Giro d'Italia in the mid 1950s.

The third section of the museum describes a brief but intense period of motorcycle development – the tri-camshaft racing twins that marked the debut of a young rider named Mike Hailwood. Next up are the singles, which achieved significant victories, despite limited means and the fact that they were derived from production models. The fifth section marks the unveiling of V-twins with bevel gears, an era best represented by two wonderful riders whose careers mark the beginning and the end of the period: Paul Smart, winner of the 1972 Imola 200, and Mike Hailwood, winner of the 1978 Tourist Trophy. Next comes a jewel of Italian engineering, the Pantah twin-cylinder (fitted with the new belt distribution engine). Conceived at the end of the 1970s, the Pantah led to many successful descendants, including the coveted TT2 and 750F1.

The story continues in 1986 with the revolutionary four-valve desmodromic engine engineered by a man whose name has become synonymous with the modern Ducati marque: Massimo Bordi. These are the bikes – first the 851 (later to become the 888) and then the current 916/996 – that make Ducati the envy of the industry and a perennial winner at World Super Bike championships. Finally, a special mention is reserved for the 1993 Supermono, a much-admired single-cylinder race bike styled by Ducati's chief stylist, Pierre Terblanche. Since its debut enthusiasts have been demanding a street version.

This passionate interest in the marque shared by journalists, collectors, riders and enthusiasts – *Ducatisti* all – has made the museum project possible. It stands as a tribute to their expertise, efforts, dedication and love for Ducati – *campione del mondo*.

A lot depends upon this man, South African Pierre Terblanche. His styling skills could ultimately make or break Ducati's plans on the big-time.

But at least Ducati have one certainty: the fact that, certainly at the current time, they seem to have no intention of building anything other than Desmo V-twins and possibly – though this is unlikely – a single. The latter revolves around Ing. Bordi's superb limited-run Supermono single. So far it has remained a racer-only, even though many have speculated upon its suitability for road use.

Working against the single is the little matter of *costs*. To build a Supermono for the street would mean a unit cost not far short of a 748 type V-twin; in other words, not much change to the buyer out of £10,000 in the UK at 1999 prices. Don't believe me?

Then go and check a few Supermono spares prices – how does £200 hit you for a cylinder head gasket? Before Cagiva sold out they had costed the project for production, and had instead come up with another machine, a 600cc Cagiva single in a Mito Evo chassis.

Apart from the four-valves-per-cylinder models that this book is all about, Ducati's other big successes during the 1990s have come from two distinct series, the SS (Super Sport) and Monster ranges.

Back at the end of the 1980s Ing. Bordi had expressed a wish that Ducati might build a multi (a four). However, this referred to the Cagiva (MV Agusta, as it is now badged) F4. Again this presents Ducati with two problems. The first is that the F4 is now part of the Cagiva empire and not TPG, in other words, Ducati. The second is that in Massimo Tamburini, Ducati have, it seems, lost their premier stylist (it was Tamburini who created the F4 and 916!). Tamburini opted to stay with Cagiva – maybe he knew something we don't. Instead it seems that Pierre Terblanche, who worked as Tamburini's assistant at CRC (Cagiva Research Centre), is the man who will be entrusted with future Ducati styling designs. In their search for increased sales, Ducati need to be able not only to increase production to previously unheard of levels, but of course they must also be able to sell the extra machines. This will mean that new motorcycles have to be even more attractive, exciting and reliable than those currently in production. The questions therefore are, can Terblanche come up with the 'must-have' bikes and can Ducati produce sufficient quantities and at a high enough quality? All three questions are vital, but at the time this book was being finished (spring 1999) it is impossible to give a definitive answer. Only time will tell.

Besides the actual design, production and quality of the motorcycles themselves, the American influence has and will bring benefits that would probably have never come otherwise. For example, there is a now a Ducati museum, a reorganized parts and after-sales service operation, clearer marketing and better publicity. Another facet of TPG's influence has been that Ducati have started to follow American Harley-Davidson down the merchandise route in areas such as clothing, accessories and even, I am sure in the future, lifestyle products. As HD know, such items, particularly in the USA, are big dollar earners that help maximize profit. And that word 'profit' is all-important to TPG; they are, after all, an investment bank! Don't be put off by that last statement, as the Americans are far more likely to make very sure that their investment pays off by in turn making sure all the cri-

teria crucial to Ducati's success are rigidly adhered to, rather than indulging in short-termist cost-cutting. Surely before investing in Ducati TPG will have done their homework, which will have told them that the Italians can produce sensuous motorcycles, but that everything else is likely to be needing, shall we say, a guiding hand.

So to sum up, I don't see Ducati's product messed about with as their governmental bosses did so badly in the mid 1970s, for example. It's very likely that Ducati will for now stick to what they are best known for – V-twins – with possibly the odd hi-tech sporting single thrown in. There will be no two-strokes, parallel twins, three- or four-cylinders and certainly no trying to take on the Japanese at their own game.

There will continue to be involvement in superbike racing (at least while they are still winning).

And as already outlined, an American-type marketing exercise, promoting both the bikes themselves and accessories, clothing and lifestyle goodies, looks likely to be adopted.

At present Ducati's motorcycle range has three firm legs: Hyper Sport (four-valve models) Super Sport and Monster. Maybe Ducati will create a fourth front. But what they certainly cannot afford to do is go backwards. Currently they are trying hard with the Sport Touring (ST2/4) models. Maybe these will prove to be the fourth and final leg to the chair. Pierre Terblanche is rumoured to be working on the 916/996 series replacement – in other words a totally new bike in much the same way the 916 replaced the 888. It will probably be this design that will either propel Ducati into the really big time as Europe's biggest bike manufacturer or put them back on the rocks of insecurity once again.

I for one will be watching developments with interest as we enter the twenty-first century.

Another vital factor is the strength of Ducati's Italian home market and its various importers around the world. The British importers, Northampton-based Moto Cinelli, are a role model for the rest of the industry – compact, efficient and enthusiastic.

1999, Ducati Corse

A new company, Ducati Corse, entirely controlled by Ducati Motor SpA, has been created with the main aim of gathering together all the sporting activities of the Ducati marque under one 'roof', guaranteeing a flexible and modern organization that is able to make the best use of the advanced technologies available today.

Ducati Corse are directed by Claudio Domenicali and are based inside the Borgo Panigale factory. Regarding sporting activity, Ducati Corse design, produce and develop competition bikes, managing and defining the sporting programmes of the official teams that in 1999 will be involved in four different championships: WSB, AMA, Super Sport and Italian Super Bike, where they will enter a new internal 'research & development' team.

On the commercial side, Ducati Corse will offer their sporting clients not only Racing and Racing Special bikes and related components, but also a complete set of services such as specialized set-up advice and know-how.

A further aim is to develop and manage the image of the Ducati marque in competition and demonstrate the capacity to evaluate the investments of partners by creating new opportunities for promotion.

Finally, it is intended to create and market a range of exclusive Ducati Corse labelled products.

Official Factory Teams	*Riders*	*Category*
Ducati Performance Team	Carl Fogarty, Troy Corser	World Super Bike Championship
Ducati Performance Team	Paolo Casoli	World Super Sport Championship
Vance & Hines Team	Anthony Gobert, Ben Bostrom	AMA Super Bike Championship
Fast By Ferracci Team	Matt Wait	AMA Super Bike Championship
Ducati Corse Team (Testing & Development)	Paolo Casoli	Italian Super Bike Championship

Ducati Corse Customer Teams	*Riders*	*Category*
Pedercini Team	Lucio Pedercini	World Super Bike Championship
R & D Racing Department Team	Doriano Romboni	World Super Bike Championship
GSE Racing Team	Neil Hodgson, Troy Bayliss	British Super Bike Championship 4 rounds WSB Championship
Rêve Red Bull Ducati Team	Sean Emmett, John Reynolds	British Super Bike championship 4 rounds WSB Championship
Ducati Dealer Team Australia	Craig Connell, Steve Martin	Australian SBK Championship
Remus Racing Team	Andreas Meklau	German Super Bike Championship

Ducati Corse Partners

Chief Sponsor   *Ducati Performance*, accessories and special parts Ducati

Other Sponsors

Shell, fuels and lubricants
Infostrada – Gruppo Olivetti, telecommunications
Dietsmann, petroleum technologies
Michelin, tyres
Magneti Marelli, ECUs and data acquisition

Termignoni, exhaust systems
USAG, tools
Brembo, braking systems
Saima Avandero, transport and logistics
Regina, chains
Accossato, handlebars
Dainese, rider leathers and team gear

DKNY, active wear
Asics, sportswear
Yuasa, batteries
Champion, spark-plugs
STM, clutch units
AFAM, crown and pinion units
Malaguti, paddock scooters

Index

Ferrari 26, 169
Ferrari, Virginio 96, 98, 114, 152
Fiat 7, 25, 116
Flory, Doug 80
Fogarty, Carl 45–8, 90, 92, 96–109, 148–9, 151–4, 157, 160, 174
Fogarty, George 92
Fogarty, Mikala 109
Ford 169
Frith, Freddie 19
Fuller, Roy 56, 71

Gandossi, Alberto 11
Garelli 86
Gasbarro, Luca 108
Ghia Design Studio 9
Gilera 86, 111
Gio.Ca.Moto 148–9
Gobert, Anthony 101, 110, 174
Goldman, David 7
Gosling, Patrick 7
Grau, Benjamin 16–17
Graves, Paul 7, 121
Green, Jeff 7, 121
Grimandi, Giorgio 59
Guggenheim Museum, New York 170

Hailwood, Mike 11, 13, 19, 170–1
Hailwood, Stan 13
Hallet, Paul 108
Halpern, Abel 119
Hannah, Bill 112
Harley-Davidson 148–9, 173
Harvey, David 7
Hockenheim circuit 85, 89, 102
Hodgson, Neil 174
Holden, Robert 78–9
Hollis, John 146
Honda 86, 90, 100, 103, 109
  CB 750 112
  CBR 600 79
  CR 125 103
  Fireblade 68
  RC 30 90, 102
  RC 45 68, 102
  VFR 750 29
  VFR 800 162–3
Husqvarna 115, 120

Imola 200 race 17, 171
ISDT 10
Isle of Man TT 19, 82–3
Ital Design Studio 19

Jackson, Doug 7
Jackson, Robert 76
Jaguar 75
Jennings, Pete 78–9
Jonas, Georgina 7

Kawasaki 63, 90, 99, 110
  GPZ1100 26
  ZX-7R 68
Kocinski, Jon 102, 107–8
Kyalami circuit 85, 89

Laguna Seca circuit 85, 89, 110
Lancia 25–6
Las Vegas Motor Speedway 110
Le Bon, Yasmin 45
Leoni, Bruno 108
Lionello, Aureliano 26
Llewellyn, Matt 48, 150
Louche, Philippe 108
Lucchiari, Mauro 108
Lucchinelli, Marco 30, 32, 88, 100, 108

Macchi MB 326 jet trainer 117
Mackenzie, Niall 97
Mandolini, Giuseppe 14
Manfredi, Davide 85
Manx Grand Prix 83
Martin, Steve 174
Massari, Pietro 85
Masters, Phil 7
MBA 86
Meakin Racing 48
Meklau, Andreas 108, 174
Mengoli, Luigi 25, 88
Merkel, Fred 90, 107
Merrill Lynch, stockbrokers 116
Mertens, Stephane 101, 108
Mid-Ohio Sports Car Course 110
Milan Show 10–11, 14, 24, 30–2, 62, 88–9, 142
Milano–Taranto 11
Mille Miglia 11
Milvio, Arnaldo 16
Minelli, Luca 108
Mini Moke 115
Minolti, Frederico 117, 119
Misano circuit 23, 27, 29, 30–1, 85, 89
Monetti, Giorgio 11
Montanari, Claudio 85
Montano, Dr Giuseppe 10, 15, 111–12
Montemaggi, Marco 170
Montjuic Park, Barcelona 16–17
Monza circuit 10–11, 80, 85, 89, 91, 160
Morisetti, Michele 85, 108
Morri, Giuseppe 62
Moto Cinelli 7, 36, 45, 47, 83, 98, 151–3, 157, 159, 173
Moto Giro 11, 171
Moto Guzzi 111

1100 Sport 144
Moto Morini 115
Moto Vecchia 36
Mugello circuit 99, 160
Munich Show 147
Museo Ducati 170–1
MV Agusta 111, 146
  F4 62, 120, 172

Nannini, Rugero 30
NCR 19, 21, 170
NEC Show, Birmingham 102
New Hampshire Int. Speedway 110
Nepoti, Giorgio 21
Norris, Brett 76
North West 200 race 46–7, 151
Nürburgring circuit 85, 89

Oran Park circuit 103
Oulton Park circuit 150
Oxford Products 44

Paget, George 81
Palmer, Geoff 57
Pani, Denis 85
Parenti, Massimo 118
Paris–Dakar Rally 22
Paul Ricard circuit 28
Pedercini, Lucio 174
Pedretti, Giuliano 30
Penegar, Jilly 7
Perlini, Maurizio 85, 108
Philips, Mark 150
Phillip Island circuit 89
Phoenix Int. Raceway 110
Pike's Peak Int. Raceway 110
Pirovano, Fabrizio 85, 101
Plater, Steve 150
Plummer, Dave 7
Plummer, Luke 7
Polen, Doug 92, 94–5, 107–8, 110
Porrozzi, Fabrizio 85, 108
Price, William S. 117

Razzano, Dante 119
Reynolds, John 174
Rhodes, Iain 7, 121
Road America 110
Road Atlanta 110
Roche, Raymond 29, 39, 90–5, 104, 107–8, 151
Romboni, Doriano 174
Rover 115
Russell, Kelvin 76
Russell, Scott 96, 99, 101, 107, 110
Rutter, Michael 45
Rutter, Tony 21, 45, 87

Seas Point Raceway 110
Senna, Ayrton 41, 72
Sheene, Barry 160

Silverstone circuit 13
Slight, Arran 100–1, 107
Smart, Paul 16, 171
Smith, Bill 48
Snetterton circuit 35
Spaggiari, Bruno 14, 16
Spairani, Fredmano 16, 112
Sports Motorcycles 19, 36, 92
Sugo circuit 89
Summerfield, Paul 83
Suzuki:
  GSX-R750 29, 68, 143
  RGV 125 69
Swedish Grand Prix 10–11

Taglioni, Ing. Fabio 10–12, 15, 19, 23, 58, 87, 111–12, 171
Tamarozzi, Ugo 9
Tamburini, Massimo 62–3, 69, 96, 120, 172
Tardozzi, Davide 85, 90, 93, 107–9
Tartarini, Leopoldo 11, 19
Tennett, Oli 7
Terblanche, Pierre 60, 62, 149, 171–3
Texas Pacific Group 7, 62, 102, 116–17, 119, 148, 169, 172–3
Three Cross Motorcycles 36, 69
Thruxton Motorcycles 79
Tibaldi, Sergio 30
Triumph Sprint ST 162
Turner, Gary 60

Ulster Grand Prix 11

Vallelunga circuit 86
Vance, Terry 110
Villa, Walter 87
Virgin Cinema Group 117
Volkswagen Golf Mark 1 113

Wait, Matt 110, 174
Wheeler, Malcolm 19, 48
Witham, James 98, 108
Williams, John 19
Willow Spring Int. Speedway 110
Woolnough, Liz 82
Woolnough, Rod 7, 82
Woolsey, David 35

Yamaha 86, 90
  TZR 125 69
  YZF 1000 Thunderace 68

Zell Chilmark Fund 116
Zell, Sam 116
Zonnedda, Franco 108